What readers are saying about *H*

"This is a good and valuable work. Like the 2003 volume entitled "Keepers -- Voices of Secular Recovery," HP is an anthology of "How I got here" stories by people who have succeeded in recovery without the 12 steps. The stories are filled with life experiences and deep feelings. They will move many a reader. There is no substitute for stories when it comes to understanding a theoretical approach. The basic formula for most of the stories follows the familiar arc of 12-step narratives: my bad life as an addict, my turnaround, my better life today. It will be easy for people steeped in 12 step habitats to relate to these stories, and it may be a revelation for such readers to grasp that the same kind of profound recovery experience can be had in a non-religious framework."

--Martin Nicolaus, Founder LifeRing Secular Recovery, author of *Empowering Your Sober Self* and *Recovery by Choice: A Workbook*

"I absolutely loved the book. Until recently, the idea and experience of secular recovery from addiction have been culturally invisible. The publication of Humanly Possible is evidence that such silence is being joyfully broken. Here are the faces and voices--the uplifting stories--of those who transformed their lives using a broad menu of secular ideas and practices. The publication of Humanly Possible is an important milestone in the history of addiction recovery. There are indeed many pathways of addiction recovery and all   are   cause   for   celebration."

--William White, Author, *Slaying the Dragon: The History of Addiction Treatment and Recovery in America*

"The stories themselves are articulately written by individuals who have thought deeply about what their challenges were, how to address them, and how to maintain the changes they made." . . . .

--A. Thomas Horvath, Phd., author *Sex, Drugs, Gambling, and Chocolate: A Workbook for Overcoming Addictions*

"It's about time! These stories show that, for many decades, people have been charting their own recoveries all over the world *outside of AA, but with the support of a mutual help group for alcohol and drug problems.* As a scientist who studies mutual help alternatives to AA, I know that people can recover from addiction by participating in secular mutual groups, and I am glad to see this book emerge. It is a needed counterpoint to the AA literature, and will most certainly inspire and help many of those who choose a secular pathway to recovery."

--Sarah E. Zemore, Ph.D. Senior Scientist, Center Associate Director, and Director of Training

Humanly Possible

Stories of Secular Recovery

Edited by Kathleen Gargan,

With Co-Editor m.k.

LifeRing Press

For additional copies of this publication, contact:

LifeRing Press
25125 Santa Clara St.
STE E, #359
Hayward, CA 94544
Tel: 800-811-4142
service@lifering.org

LifeRing Books can be purchased at Amazon or the LifeRing Bookstore at www.lifering.org/bookstore.

Bulk orders can be sent to publisher@lifering.org

ISBN: 978-0-578-50370-7

PREFACE……………………………………..………………….. i
ACKNOWLEDGMENTS……,………………………………….... iv
Story 1 - Closing the Circuit, by Njon Sanders……………….. 1
Story 2 - An Old Man Grows Up, by Mike K……………………. 7
Story 3 - My Story, by Craig Whalley…………………………... 16
Story 4 - Self-Empowered, by Adam Sledd…………………….. 24
Story 5 - The Conversation, by John Cutaia…………………… 28
Story 6 - Looking Back, by Tom Jarrell…………………………. 33
Story 7 - I Guess I Had Seen Too Many Movies, by Anonymous 38
Story 8 - It's Never Too Late to Get a Life, by Nancy Corbett… 44
Story 9 – Badassery, by Dennis Meeks…………………………. 49
Story 10 – Powerlessness, by Philip Henderson………..……….. 52
Story 11 - Magic Has to Happen Somehow, by Bobbi Campbell... 53
Story 12 - I Am Not an Alcoholic!, by Catherine Henley…....….. 64
Story 13 – Friendship, by D.L.H…………..…………..……..….. 72
Story 14 - My Recovery Story, by Mary Lee Peterson…………... 78
Story 15 - Magical Mystery Tour, by Richard Campbell……......... 80
Story 16 - Finding My Power, by Mary S………………………...... 93
Story 17 - My Journey Started on a Stretcher, by Katie Gallagher.. 102
Story 18 - I Was Ten, by Steve Snyder……………..……….....….. 113
Story 19 - etude-itude, by m.k……..…………………………….... 114
Story 20 - Flight to Sobriety, by Hilary…………………………... 117
Story 21 - A Prisoner Friend, by Tim Reith………….…...……….. 120
Story 22 - The Long and Winding Road, by Robert Stump…….... 125
Story 23 - Making Sense of It All Twelve Years On, by James Ringland. 125
Story 24 - I Call Myself Sober, by Byron Kerr………………….. 136
Story 25 - Chemistry 101: Re-balancing the Equation, by m.k….. 140
Story 26 - Lost (and Found) in Margaritaville, by Patricia Gauss.. 142
Story 27 - Sober in Sapporo, by CA Edington…..……………..... 148
Story 28 - Three SMART Stories…………………………..…..…. 161
Story 29 - Perry Street Workshop, by John L………..……….….. 180
CONTRIBUTORS………………………………………….......….. 187

PREFACE

"Narration is the quintessential form of customary knowledge"
Jean-Francois Lyotard

"We tell ourselves stories in order to live."
- Joan Didion

Stories are said to be as necessary to humankind as food and shelter and love. They compel, entertain and delight us; they soothe our fears and give shape to our hopes and dreams. They are like mirrors where we recognize ourselves in the struggles of champions and monsters alike. They overcome the distances between us by allowing us to identify with each other. These are some of the ways that narrative gives meaning to lives.

For those of us who seek relief from addiction, stories are essential in a concrete way. Narrative is a kind of evidence, and as such it has power; and power is famously assumed to be lacking for people with addictions. The power of narrative evidence is in its capacity to inspire belief in the possibility of recovery.

Certainly, as anecdotal evidence, narrative does not carry the weight of rigorous scientific studies. But the experimental study of addiction has thus far not brought the kind of relief that would make other kinds of evidence unnecessary. This slow progress may be the result of the extraordinarily complicated nature of addiction, involving, as it does, both the body and more illusively, the mind. It may be the result of moral and political prejudice. In either case, in the absence of a conclusive medical explanation of addiction, narrative provides strong evidence for demonstrating the varied "mechanics" of secular recovery.

The stories offered in this volume, of individuals living free of addictions by means of purely secular ideas, tools and practices provide powerful testimony that what was not long ago thought to be possible only by means of supernatural intervention, is also "humanly" possible. This volume was inspired by the need for such evidence. Without it, countless people whose worldview is strictly secular, have had little basis for believing that they might live according to their own conscience and be free of addiction at the same time.

According to Aristotle and other students of rhetoric, individual stories can often be tracked according to the following universal structure of drama: first, the rising action, which portrays a conflict between a protagonist and an antagonist, then a crisis or turning point, and finally a resolution. Even if life itself is rarely so clearly organized, this dramatic structure has proven useful, and often characteristic of the lives of many recovering people.

Many of the stories in this volume are written by people who have recovered with the help of tools learned in part from LifeRing Secular Recovery. They are not professional writers, but their stories follow the universal structure of drama. The rising action in many LifeRing stories describes a progressive path to recovery in terms of a give and take between a Sober Self and an Addicted Self. The turning point in many of our stories involves making peace between the Sober Self and the Addicted Self. The resolution is accomplished by taking action on behalf of the Sober Self which we believe exists in every person who is suffering from active addiction. It is the Sober Self within us all, that human sized protagonist, living in a fully natural world, that we learn to nourish as the hero in ourselves and each other in LifeRing. LifeRing and other secular recovery organizations are composed of sober selves joining together to affirm and celebrate their sobriety.

The word secular derives from the latin *seculum* meaning "of *this* time or age". Those of us in secular recovery do indeed conduct our lives, not on the basis of what was believed at an earlier time, or on what may happen in another world after we die, but according to what is known thus far by means of practical evidence. This means that our stories describe what has worked for us from the ideas, tools and practices that derive from the natural world, here and now. It is our hope that this volume might contribute to the mounting evidence that secular recovery is possible for those who need it.

Kathleen Gargan

April 21, 2019

Denver, Colorado

ACKNOWLEDGMENTS

First, a word about the editing choices that were made for this book. All stories submitted were accepted for publication here. Stories were very lightly edited. Changes were made only to ensure the clarity of the narrative. Great care was taken to preserve the original voices of the authors.

I wish to thank the following people for their support, encouragement and hard work:

Most important, thanks to those of you who, though not professional writers, took the time and the effort to put your stories into writing. You are helping countless others to believe in the possibility of a life free from addiction without the sacrifice of a secular worldview.

I am grateful to m.k. who sat with me for long hours reading stories aloud and parsing sentences for a full half of the stories in this book. Thanks to Craig Whalley, for his moral support and editing and proofreading help. Thanks to Rosemary Haskell, also for much valued moral support and for proofreading many stories. Thanks to Chet Gardiner, Rick Thompson and Byron Kerr, for proofreading. Special thanks to Robert Stump for many hours of diligent work in converting files and formatting.

Finally, thanks to the LifeRing Board of Directors for their patience for the four years of this book's development.

"The Perry St. Workshop" is reprinted here courtesy of John Lauritsen, author of *A Freethinker in Alcoholics Anonymous* (2014)

Cover design by Sue Campbell.

Kathleen Gargan

Denver, Colorado

April 2019

Story 1

Closing the Circuit
by Njon Sanders

Sobriety: noun so·bri·ety \səə-ˈbrī-əə-tē, sō-\ the state of being sober.

synonyms: soberness, clear-headedness

A child of the 70s, I was the queer, ethnically ambiguous kid in middle-class suburban Ohio where residents coexisted in largely separate but unequal circles that interacted but did not, as a rule, overlap. I became an adept chameleon, a master of assimilation, and walked in many of these circles as an associate member. I was popular for my jokes and friendliness; a byproduct of my paralyzing fear of being "othered". My social anxiety and unshakeable imposter syndrome led to acting out in ways that often appeared either brave or, just stupid. I learned to self-medicate and hide my insecurity, employing "humor" and mirroring the bully-like behavior I was subjected to. I was a damaged and confused kid.

In the late 80's, I became acutely aware of the term "sobriety" when most of my school friends were sent to rehab for addiction issues. Despite my limited but ambitious use of alcohol and drugs, I felt that I too must have these same problems, so I followed my friends into "recovery". Back then, in my area, there was only one known path to recovery.

Surprisingly, sobriety remains widely viewed as being synonymous with abstinence and I heard testimony of its power at the meetings I attended daily. I was instructed to have blind respect for any individual who had amassed more abstinence than I. I was instructed to rely on these people for guidance, or risk immediate death, because of my addiction which was anthropomorphized and assigned human powers such as "doing pushups out in the parking

1

lot" while I got my recovery on in the safety of smoky church basements. I was told that "my best thinking got me to where I was" so I'd better surrender to the power of an unseen something greater than myself and the wisdom of the addicts who showed up before me. My "failure" as a person was seen as an ego problem.

Meetings consisted of ten to fifteen minutes of repetitive opening credits followed by the speaker. One-upmanship was king. Drunkalogues and horror stories were the interesting parts of the shares. These were typically followed with a standard closing like "and then I found sobriety and now everything is awesome! Comments...?" My mind would be screaming: "But everyone knows you're still cheating on your wife and you're still pretty much an asshole!" The frequent, institutionalized reminders that I was not worthy of independent or intelligent thought, though, kept me from voicing these irrelevant observations; my "disease talking".

At nearly three years of sustained abstinence, I still felt like an impostor. My earnest attempts at surrender and turning my life over to "the sky ghosts" had resulted only in a raw sense of inadequacy which I no longer self-medicated. My inside voice declared "THIS IS BULLSHIT!!" while I cursed myself for my inability to follow in the footsteps of my peers, who could surrender and who embraced their powerlessness. This led to my clinical diagnosis of "the Fuckits".

At eighteen years old, I, along with a peer who shared my sense of hopelessness, decided to at least have some fun in our youthful addiction as opposed to maintaining the constant self-flagellation that was integral to the recovery lifestyle of the day. Out of pure selfishness, we convinced a third member to flee with us. We each dove in head-first and started down roads toward what felt like the typical heavy drinking associated with young adulthood and its new-found freedoms.

Inevitably, I followed the standard substance use progression, preemptively treating pain, discomfort, or the potential of either, by numbing my senses with alcohol, cocaine or whatever was handy. My use became daily in my mid-twenties and by my thirties had

2

developed into a severe physical addiction. In retrospect, I'd developed a daily routine to disguise my use to the outside world, while I focused on the next fix. It became a second (but much more important) job. Traveling became a logistical nightmare!

As my addiction advanced and further manifested itself, it surpassed my ability to conceal it. It became clear that the time for me to cut back or stop had indeed arrived and I knew I needed help. I'd recently quit smoking cigarettes and felt more in control of myself and my consumption so I decided I could man-up and do whatever was required of me to not pick up another drink or drug.

My goal as I understood it was, again, the abstinence commonly equated with sobriety. I knew from my experience years before that everything wouldn't just magically be perfect once I quit, but the shame and insecurity I felt in my last attempt held the attraction as the lesser of two evils when compared to my physical deterioration, fear of getting caught, and heightened sense of mortality.

Employing my best thinking, I found an outpatient rehab that met my requirements for autonomy, and which felt the least evangelical. My intake counselor discussed medical assistance by means of prescription drugs to ease my withdrawal symptoms. I opted-out but was pleased to know that this existed. She also offered me literature from several mutual support organizations. This was a bit shocking to me, as I had assumed that I would be required to surrender to the restrictive recovery lifestyle I'd known previously.

I was also skeptical of what I imagined these hippy-dippy-touchy-feely- kumbaya-bullshit meetings must be like. I had nothing to lose though, so I invited a friend from work to come to my first LifeRing meeting with me. I was surprised that upon my arrival, a friendly conversation about some current world event was going on instead of the expected repetitive litany. I waited for the instruction to label myself as an addict/alcoholic/new member/failure but that never happened. We went around the circle, each talking about our last week in recovery and any potential challenges or milestones in the coming week. This was just like process group in treatment!! I could wrap my mind around this! The group also seemed oddly

3

unconcerned with scoring people by the number of days of abstinence. I was allowed and even encouraged to give feedback, based on my experience. The conversation was support-focused, and no one micromanaged the conversation or got chewed-out. Holy Cow! It was like speaking with adults!

That weekend, I went to another LifeRing meeting which has since become my weekly reset button. I quickly bonded with a core group of regulars and started to relearn the social skills needed to navigate friendly relationships without chemical "embellishment". My new friends knew only my sober persona. They supported me and came to me for support in their times of need. This only encouraged me to become more the person they saw and helped me slowly let go of the unworthy drunk identity I instinctively clung to.

The initial period of abstinence allowed, and sometimes forced, me to feel the feelings I'd been avoiding for decades and in turn, afforded me a sense of comfort in the vulnerability I shared with my peers and my therapist. I had not imagined this possible. I discovered I no longer dreaded going to meetings as in my previous attempt. I looked forward to going to recovery meetings where I'd not only see my friends but could test my newfound honesty in a supportive environment. I learned that being honest with myself and caring for myself were both possible and productive.

I was riding the proverbial pink cloud that the recovery community generally views as an ephemeral, artificial and temporary. In this state, my ability to make genuine reciprocal connections with people and to have meaningful conversations with them felt like a superpower.

Through attending meetings and spending time with my sober friends, the anxiety surrounding social situations and situational acceptance slowly diminished. I became increasingly able to take my new self-confidence and vulnerability out of the meeting rooms and into the "real world". As I suspected, the outside world isn't typically as supportive as meeting rooms. Using my superpowers of honesty and concern for others, however, attracted groups of like-minded people whose natural instinct had become (wait for it…) honesty and

4

support (I know, right?!?!)

"My sobriety goals may not look like yours and I won't try to superimpose my ideas on you" replaced "Well, it works if you work it" and "This was good enough for me". Self-empowerment replaced Surrender. The very concepts of surrender and letting go remain as baffling and foreign to me today as they did decades ago. The abuse of these precepts has been demonstrated in and out of the recovery community time and time again. Previously I'd been incapable making the apparently necessary paradigm shift in my belief system; the one that would cement my place with my peers in recovery. This time however, I was made to feel included and given the support I needed to determine the best path for myself as a participant and not a passenger waiting for things to happen.

These days, while the pink cloud no longer has that new-car smell, I'm still proudly riding it. I haven't experienced the proverbial "lightbulb moment" when shit just "gets good". That said, it's been more like a string of tiny fairy lights that represent ongoing growth and progress. These, in conjunction with the new connections I'm fostering, my determination, and perseverance are what keep me moving forward on my journey of self-improvement.

Sobriety itself has taken on a whole new meaning to me in recent years. I used to equate it with abstinence. I've reached the conclusion that for me, abstinence is merely the necessary prerequisite tool that I use to achieve sobriety. Sobriety is, to me, the sense of clarity that facilitates forward momentum and personal growth. It's most noticeable when I feel that I'm choosing a good path for myself and making a positive and honest impact (or when I catch myself not doing so and I course-correct).

Discomfort and fear sometimes feed the old feelings of self-loathing. So, relapse for me is not the act of picking up a drink or drug. It's the process of allowing these former instincts to convince me that discomfort is pain, and that pain is never-ending or unbearable. It's the panicked urgency in avoiding or postponing them immediately and at any cost. I realize that this is just my lizard brain trying to help me avoid stress, but in the long run, for me, it's just plain flawed thinking.

Abstinence remains an extremely important tool in my recovery toolbox, but it is no longer the goal. The inflexible and finite qualities of this concept revealed themselves very early, proving it an inadequate success metric. The substance use factor of my time in crisis was a secondary disorder, exacerbated by of my underlying, undiagnosed anxiety and negative self-perception. Addressing my primary issues, in conjunction with my makeshift remedies has negated the need for me to struggle with the consequences of either. With the support of my recovery family, abstinence came surprisingly easy for me. This, again, has enabled me to take the offensive in addressing the entirety of my behavioral health.

Today, I continue a regimen that includes my weekly reset meeting. I use the meeting primarily as a sounding board. I find that verbalizing my experiences and thoughts forces me to better formulate and acknowledge them on a more honest level. It pushes me to a greater level of conscious integrity with myself. Facilitating meetings and volunteering in other capacities helps me to continue to practice making the honest connections that promote my reintegration.

Many wise people around me have described a cumulative nature of sobriety. This means that the sober connections we make have a net positive impact on our lives and that no incident, bad choice, or mistake can take those away from us. Simply put, recovery cannot be measured in days abstinent. One does not become "more sober" simply by accumulating a greater number of consecutive, abstinent days. The concept of sobriety being measurable to any single metric is, to me, unhelpful. In my opinion, it's up to us as individuals to decide what our recovery should look like. Attempting to compare or quantify these individual definitions and concepts seems a fool's errand.

My hope for you, if you are reading this, is that you may find some inspiration and feel empowered to find the kind of support that you are comfortable with. You have the power to formulate paths to reach you goals, whatever they might be!

Story 2

An Old Man Grows Up
by Mike K.

Last week Henry died. He ended a year's sobriety by deciding to have a few drinks and he started to hemorrhage internally. The hospital could not pump blood into him fast enough, so his organs shut down and he died. We saw Henry now and then around meetings and he always seemed laid back and quiet. One of his friends told us, "Henry did drink now and then, and this time was once too often. Henry is no longer with us." The body has been sent back to Arkansas where Henry has some family, but we don't even know where to send flowers.

Meanwhile, after being in prison since 1980 and going through a total of 11 Parole Board Hearings, Perry has been found suitable for parole by the Parole Board in California. In 1979, he was drunk, and he killed a guy over a woman. He is now 59 years old and he has been sober since 1982 which is the last time he got into any trouble. After his first two years inside, he was celled-up with a famous cooker of Pruno and he had to consume his product just to convince the customers that it was drinkable. The guards shut down the cookery and Perry has been clean and sober and a model prisoner ever since.

I am between Henry and Perry in my experience with sobriety. Alcohol had been a sometimes dance partner for me since I was 15 years old and attending a small, high pressure prep school where there were 10 of us in a class. Our graduation class was written up in *Time* magazine as some sort of freak show with seven of us going to Harvard, one to Wesleyan in Connecticut, one exchange student returning home to New Zealand, and one going to the University of Texas. No reader of that issue of *Time* was able to see the wreckage inside the eight of those boys, boys who had been through four years at that school and missed their adolescence altogether.

After a long career in industrial marketing and business management, five years ago I retired at the age of 72. For the final decade of that career, my wife and I formed our own consulting company and we had a solid international business that gave me great freedom to pick my travel and set my agenda. Actually while our business was often solid, I was occasionally liquid leading to foggy. The plusses in my reputation and performance must have outweighed the minuses because I continued to produce and to earn, but the minuses were legendary, and they all involved booze in one way or another.

Retiring is traumatic. I was tired and ready to stop working, but the idea that I would not be able to earn my way out of whatever hole I dug was a terrifying prospect. With no structure and no accountability, I floundered. The first drink got earlier in the afternoon and almost all of the drinks got more secret.

Then my mother started to fail. She was 102 and staying in an assisted living in the same town where she had lived for the previous 43 years. My father had died 36 years earlier, and after his death, Mother earned a real estate license and graduated from the local community college at the age of 82. She had promised to stop driving when she reached 99 but she told me as long as the car was at her house, she was afraid she would keep driving it. So, I bought the car. She went into an assisted living home before she turned 100 because she was falling and secretly getting afraid to live alone in her house. But she was healthy and alert and quickly set a tone of lively interaction in her new home. Everybody in that town knew Pauline and took as fact that she was the last resort whenever there was any question that needed answering. She was a wordsmith and she prided herself on never lying … ever. One day, my brother called to say that Mother had had a small stroke. We knew she had a living will with medical instructions to refuse any artificial life saving measures. We agreed that there seemed to be no choice other than to put Mother into hospice care and let her die.

Many years earlier when my father was dying, my first wife was in a psychiatric hospital where I had admitted her after another of her suicide attempts. She had lost patience with the overdose of pills she had taken while sitting in our car and had decided instead to drive into a bridge support. But she had been going only fast enough to total the car and bring the police to haul her in. The hospital pumped her stomach and turned her over to me. She was not hurt physically, but I had to keep her at home overnight until I could get her checked into the psych ward the next morning.

So, as my father was dying, I would be at the one hospital outside the intensive care ward waiting for the few minutes I could see my father each hour while my wife would be calling me on the public pay phone in the waiting room, screaming at me to get her out of the locked ward in the hospital where she was. When it was all over, and my father had died, and I had signed for the release of my wife against medical advice … I told a friend I would never allow myself to be in such an impossible situation again. He said, "How are you going to manage that?"

Now it was my mother who was dying. My second wife is a generous and empathetic woman who had somehow stayed on my side and loved me even after 30 years of being married to me and to my drinking. My wife does not like to travel at all and certainly not on the interstate highways between our house and Mother's town, a two-hour drive away. But when I told her about Mother's condition, the plan for hospice, and that I needed to be with Mother and my brother as we made the arrangements and waited for the inevitable end, my wife said she wanted to go along with me and would stay as long as we needed to stay. We were to leave the next morning .

That afternoon I started to drink. I had no specific thoughts about a cause or a purpose or a consequence. I just started to drink. At that time in our retirement my wife and I would watch the news together at 6 p.m. and each of us would have one drink. By then, I had switched from dark whiskey to clear booze so the strength of my drink was a mystery and usually I would get a head start on our time together. On that evening I was truly and obviously drunk when I joined my wife to watch the news. She told me to just go to bed and for some reason I did exactly that. The next morning, she said she could not go with me, that I should go ahead and deal with what I had to do, and we would sort ourselves out afterward. She wanted no discussion past my acceptance that she simply could not be around me. So, I went.

I got to the assisted living home to meet my brother and the hospice to find that mother had rallied. She was in a wheelchair and perky but she still could not speak. So, hospice was cancelled. As Mother gained some speech over the next few days, she decided she did want a feeding tube and nourishment, so we did that. But the downward spiral had begun, and she died a couple of days later at 102 years and 9 months old.

I collected my stuff and myself and started driving home. While I had been away, I had kept my wife informed about Mother's progression and now I called to tell her I was on my way home. She said, "Something is going to have to change. And I mean really change, not just words or promises but real change." I said, "I know it. I am going to be able to tell you what that change will be and how I will do it by the time I get home." As I said those words, I knew that for the first time I was sincerely committing to the change I had mouthed so often before. I had said it on and off for over 50 years, but it never really came from deep inside me. It had been thoroughly terrifying, but I had been employing surface tactics to deflect surface pressures and get past surface unpleasantness for all that time. My mother had died, and I had hurt my wife. It was time to honor both of them and start growing up at last. This time I knew I was saying it to myself and not just to an audience.

Why was this time different?

Had the loss of one of the amazing women in my life somehow gotten my attention and lead me to realize I wanted to fight to keep the central, most important one, my wife?

Had my fear of drinking and its effects outgrown the fear that fueled my drinking?

Had I finally gone so far in selfish destructive behavior that even I could not stand it?

Was my embarrassment and shame more than I could cover up?

Was I looking down a tunnel of dark loneliness and ebbing life and refusing to go?

Probably some of all the above was at work.

When I got home, I told my wife I would stop drinking no matter what it took. I made an appointment with the counselor I had been seeing for a couple of years. and he was amused that I had finally decided to be serious about how much damage booze was doing in my life. He did suggest a club in the area that hosts 12-step meetings and he did endorse Alcoholics Anonymous. I went even though I had long resisted AA for many uninformed reasons. I had been sure that the religiosity and reliance on God were formulaic rituals that would repel me. Also, I was increasingly hidden from others and from myself, so joining anything sounded excruciating. And I was 72 years old so how was I going to start something I knew nothing about? But three weeks after coming back from my mother's death and promising my wife and myself I would do anything to avoid drinking, I went to my first AA meeting.

It wasn't bad. People were nice enough and the second week I announced my 30 days of sobriety and a guy gave me a coin. There was a sense that maybe I could adopt an attitude of being sober. Of course, I started taking notes and thinking I could capture everything and everybody and then own them as experiences and then memories. Of course, I immediately began sniffing around for some recognition and approval of the great changes in me. But I was sober.

My recovery branched out from there. In fact, AA says take what works for you and make your own program just as LifeRing says make your own plan of recovery. As an example, I never got a sponsor because I thought that would make my efforts at sobriety the primary job of someone else and I was not going to take that chance. Besides, my experience is that authority and I have not been compatible. Next, I started to experiment with reading and thinking and looking at alternative paths in sobriety. And for once I was accumulating some knowledge without planning to be tested on it, just knowledge to be used to build a base for myself without staying poised to defend it or prove it or flaunt it. There was a comfort to that stage and maybe it was because I began to realize that I did not have to be afraid. As I look back, that is surprising because it was a very real fear that forced me to commit to sobriety. I was paying attention to what I was doing and not to the fear that had driven me to it.

I found on-line non-religious and anti-religious groups: AA Agnostic, AA Atheists and Agnostics, Free Thinkers, Sober Friends, and finally LifeRing. I have participated in all of them while they were active, and I have read extensively in the recovery literature. I had always been interested in religion as a topic of academic attention and I had even attended some courses at the Harvard Divinity School when I was an undergraduate at the College. Buddhism attracted me too, as it seemed to raise so much of the AA program to an ancient and revered philosophical level, so I consumed various presentations of Eastern humanistic thought. My major in college was The History and Literature of the Renaissance and Reformation, so looking at human society with an eye to religious themes was natural to me. I was not giving my mind away by going to AA meetings. I was gaining the simple social interaction that had been missing in my life.

Here is the classic definition of *secular*: *Of or relating to worldly things or to things that are not regarded as religious, spiritual, or sacred: temporal secular interests. Not pertaining to or connected with religion (opposed to sacred)*

My recovery is secular as I understand the concept. My only dispute with the classical definitions above is the exclusion of "spiritual" in the first definition. My growth and recovery from addiction require spiritual work because they require a change in that unseen part of me that makes me who I am and not interchangeable with any other human. That unseen part of me is my spirit. So, while my recovery is secular and spiritual, it is definitely not religious. Still, I do not put myself in opposition to anyone who has a recovery plan that works for him or her, as long as that plan does not include imposing itself on anyone else.

I will not participate in any group that does not willingly accept the wide range of beliefs and non-beliefs among other members of the group. If anyone insists that god has a capital "g" and there is only one god that rules all our separate and individual understanding I object, directly and unambiguously.

I have close friendships in AA groups that I don't think on-line interaction can provide. And I knew when I retired, that human interaction, or the lack of it, would be a problem in my new life. This summer I will go on my third float trip on a spring fed stream in the Ozark foothills where some 130 sober guys camp outside, float canoes down the river, eat meals they prepare, and enjoy the natural wonders of the outdoors.

"The only requirement for membership [in AA] is the desire to stop drinking." That statement by itself assures me that I can treat my AA participation as a secular pursuit. Or I read the words of Bill Wilson himself from 1961, "in AA's first years I all but ruined the whole undertaking with this sort of unconscious arrogance. God as I understood Him had to be for everybody. Sometimes my aggression was subtle and sometimes it was crude. But either way it was damaging — perhaps fatally so — to numbers of non-believers."

When the owner of the last company where I was an employee promoted me to president of the company, I was into waters over my head particularly in matters of financial management. My wife had earned an M.B.A. early in our marriage and after my promotion, she proposed that she serve as a consultant without pay to help me and the company for a period of time to let the owners gain confidence in her value. Before long the company hired her to the position of Vice President of Finance and Administration so she and I could become professional managers of the company. That was a difficult time. We had not defined my alcoholism yet and my resentment at the intrusion on my drinking and isolation was an unacknowledged stress in our relationship. But she was rigorous about doing our work well and professionally even in an environment toxic to her.

And now my wife is as close to a sponsor in AA terms as I have. She is my sounding board on any signs I may show of accumulating tension because she knows me so well. We are learning how to be together, as sources of strength for each other. I am still living sober for me first because I accept that it cannot be done unless I do it for myself first. But the primary resource in that sobriety is my wife. She is letting me grow up from being a teenager, a place where I was stuck for about 55 years. She believed in the better me before I was willing to admit that it might actually exist.

Among my recovery tools, those needed handholds on sobriety, I have one that is especially valuable to me. There is a program called the Corrections Communications Services, run under the auspices of the AA General Services Office. The Corrections Communications Services group supplies the names of men in prison who area asking for an alcoholic "on the outside" who will correspond with them. I got some names of individuals through that service four years ago and started writing to them. They are men who have taken the initiative to request an alcoholic correspondent and who are in prison at least three states away so there is no likelihood of finding them on my doorstep when they get released. Some of them answer the first letter, some don't. Some are steady and answer every letter promptly, some write only occasionally. When the flow of letters slows to an unsatisfactory trickle I send for more names. Every week I get one or two letters from men who are in prison, men who want a contact with whom to share thoughts and experiences. I write them letters that try to connect with them at a human level without letting the wrenching difference between our situations get in the way. They want to write about what they believe, and they ask what I believe. In this correspondence I exercise my new-found muscles of honesty and I exert effort to answer without pretense.

One of the fellows I corresponded with was in prison in South Dakota and many of the inmates there were Native Americans. They objected to the use of the "god" concept when my friend tried to start a new AA meeting at the prison. We checked with the AA General Services Office and learned there is a special desk dedicated to the application of AA principles in the Native American community. My correspondent now uses "the great spirit" in place of "a god of our understanding" and this meeting is growing and helping the folks who attend it.

When I read and write these letters, I am constantly reminded of the blessings of the freedom I have and the assumed responsibility to use that freedom well – or at the very least with an appreciation that it is there.

At the beginning of my story I mentioned Perry. He is among the first men I contacted in the Corrections Communication Service and we have written every week for four years. Maybe Governor Brown will reverse the Parole Board finding in favor of Perry or maybe he will let it stand. Either way, Perry says he is able to accept that reality and he shows me a standard of peace that I could never have imagined on my own. I have never felt the beauty and urgency of sobriety more than when I sit down to correspond with prison inmates from the freedom of my own desk in my own house.

I have not had a drink since that day I told my wife I knew things had to change as I drove back from being with my mother when she died. Free at last feels good.

Story 3

My Story
by Craig Whalley

The idea of "hitting bottom" has always seemed silly to me. I see life as more of a maze of at least three dimensions in which we strive to travel from the bottom to the top and from the edge to the center. Often, a move upward has the perverse effect of pushing us closer to an edge, and that might require a step or two downward in order to move back towards the center. In other words, life is too complex to view it as a simple ladder upon which we travel up or down.

That said, I must admit that my own life was heading down and towards the outer edge by 1999. I was twice-divorced, obese, deeply in debt, socially isolated, hypertensive, depressed, owning a business with declining sales, and drinking large quantities of beer and wine daily. I was still functional much of each day but was gradually becoming less so. I was perfectly aware that my drinking was at the heart of most of my problems and that quitting was at the heart of making things better. "Denial," at least in that simple sense, had vanished long before.

I had quit on my own for significant periods of time previously, but it had become harder and harder to sustain the idea that I could solve my drinking problem on my own. So I began to plan for help. To me, back then, as to almost everyone even now, "getting help" with a drinking problem started and ended with AA. Alcoholics Anonymous was embedded in the public consciousness as the place to go for dealing with alcoholism.

But I owned a bookstore and had had the opportunity to skim through copies of the "Big Book" of AA. What I read made me exceedingly uncomfortable. First of all, there was the writing style, very much a product of a 1930's white American Protestant small-town mindset. I'm no book-snob; I read lots of books that lack literary merit. But this book had the pompous, self-congratulatory air

16

of those men (and they are almost always men) who believe that self-education is more valuable than "book learning." Much of it was written in the first-person plural ("we learned that we ....") which always makes my skin crawl a little, although maybe that's just me.

But okay, it was a 60-year-old book and I could try to overlook the distancing effect that had on me. After all, many great classics of literature were written in what now seems a stilted and constrained style. But then there was the religion. It took 30 seconds or less to realize that 'Higher Power' meant "God," and a decidedly Christian god at that. No matter how vehemently this is denied by AA believers, nothing could be clearer. And while I had been raised Christian and confirmed in the Congregational Church and had been a believer into my 20's, I no longer accepted the god stuff as anything except instructive mythology. Most of the 12 steps -- maybe all of them -- are directly or indirectly related to Protestant Christian beliefs widely held in the era in which it was written (and still held today by millions). How could I get what I needed to quit drinking if it came in a package of what felt to me like Christian Evangelism?

Still, I thought, maybe ... but then I read the Steps. Well, I read the First Step, which I couldn't get passed. It's a declaration of an addict's powerlessness over addiction. Now, I'm no strong-willed manly man who carries a gun while he's playing tackle football against a team of evil-doers. I was just a small-town businessman, not Warren Buffett. But "powerless"? Call me arrogant, but I had built my business from scratch, learning as I went, all by myself. Every day brought challenges that I had to meet. I wasn't doing well on the drinking front and my life was, in fact, a mess, but I sure wasn't going to start my recovery by declaring my total weakness or, worse, blaming my own flawed character.

So that was my dilemma: which was worse, drinking or buying into the 12-step approach? I was leaning towards the former, but then decided that I couldn't be the only person in the world who had trouble viewing the 12 steps as any sort of adequate solution for my problem. So I began searching on Google for alternatives. At first, I had poor success -- search terms that included AA produced innumerable sites for AA believers. The Google algorithms have, I'm sure, improved since then, but it was highly discouraging at first. And, of course, being an active addict, my enthusiasm for searching would fade quickly after a couple of failures.

After a few weeks of intermittent effort, I hit on the search term that saved me: "secular." That word was very rare in the AA world, but often is used in alternative groups, most prominently by LifeRing Secular Recovery. So, I found LifeRing's website and immediately felt a vast sense of relief. There were others like me!

Even on the opening page of the website, it was abundantly clear what the differences were with AA. I wasn't powerless! I just needed to have my own power nurtured and supported. Addiction wasn't a spiritual problem! Call it a disease if you want, or a condition, and trace it to genetics or psychology or learned behavior or childhood trauma, but it didn't come from some spiritual or character weakness, and it wasn't going to be cured by divine intervention. And the writers on the website were simply better writers than the authors of the Big Book. I didn't have to turn off my brain and accept a bunch of beliefs and approaches that, if examined at all closely, didn't seem reality-based. And the use of far fewer slogans was a big plus (I recently read a delicious line: "slogans are empty suits draped on the corpse of an idea").

I also found Rational Recovery on the internet, which seemed intriguing. But it didn't offer ongoing involvement, or much depth of thought and I felt pretty certain that their approach was too limited in scope and in potential for real involvement for what I wanted.

But LifeRing sounded like it was designed with me in mind! Except, that is, that there were no LifeRing support meetings anywhere near my small Washington State town. But they did offer online support, and, on impulse, I joined LSRmail, a private email group. Email groups ("listservs") are a way of sending emails to a group address and having it go to all other members of the group, as do all replies. Membership has to be approved by the group moderator, which is intended to keep spammers and troublemakers

18

out while preserving confidentiality. I found the email group format to be perfect for someone like me. I'm pretty introverted and shy and I quickly realized that I absorbed a lot more from reading than from listening and wrote better than I spoke. The other people in LSRmail were kind and intelligent and I very quickly felt like I'd become an accepted and supported member of the group.

This is the point in my story where everything should have come together with a great transformation and healing after a laying-on of secular hands. The "support" piece of the puzzle was in place! All that was needed was for me to grab hold and leap into recovery.

But it wasn't enough for me. Repeated efforts to actually quit drinking, as opposed to talking about quitting or wanting to quit, met with failure. My life by this point was teetering on the brink of financial ruin and I made the classic addict mistake of convincing myself that it was the anxiety I felt that was preventing me from making the jump to sobriety. My feelings were causing the drinking, I reasoned, rather than the other way around. Needless to say, my repeated failures were very discouraging. Maybe, I thought, there was something to that "powerlessness" stuff. Maybe I really couldn't quit, with or without a support group.

Dismayed, I dropped out of the email group after several months. I did keep in touch with a couple of friends I had made there (both living thousands of miles away from me) and we wrote back and forth frequently. Only rarely was sobriety discussed -- the focus was much more on "normal" friend talk, though with more depth than I was used to. I wasn't so far gone that I couldn't carry on a friendship, but they were sober, and I wasn't and that rankled - what did they know that I didn't? Not that I felt able to ask them. If I had, I think they would have said they didn't know of anything.

Looking back now, I think I know the answer. I think they simply valued sobriety more highly than I did at that time. It was more important to them than anything else and so they had been willing to change the things in their lives that needed changing in order to sustain their sobriety. LifeRing speaks of the "Sobriety Priority," meaning simply that sobriety has to take precedence over just about everything else in your life. I could give lip-service to that idea, but in reality, I hadn't understood it at all.

What would you do for love? Would you move to a foreign country to be with your lover? Would you quit your job? Leave your friends? Love is a powerful force and can compel us to make incredible changes. Now, how about sobriety? Will you give up your (hard-drinking) friends for it? Leave a stressful job? Learn how to deal differently with your emotions? In other words, would you make the changes in your life necessary to bring about lasting sobriety? It was, clearly, a question I had avoided asking myself. Or I had finessed the question by a stubborn belief that my issues were beyond my ability to control.

My desire to become sober had limits that I kept hidden from myself. It wasn't denial of my drinking problem -- I knew perfectly well that I was addicted -- but denial of the extent of the changes that I needed to make. All approaches to addiction recovery attempt to instill a desire for sobriety that exceeds the desire to drink or use. Religious approaches want you to open your heart to a Higher Power who will reach inside you and make the necessary changes. That approach was not available to me. Regardless of what many sincerely believe, I do not accept the existence of a spiritual "Higher Power" able to do that, and I can no more open my heart to a supernatural force than I can look for Santa Claus to appear on Christmas Eve. The only higher power in my life was the massive pile of debt I faced.

Time passed. I awoke on the morning of Jan. 1, 2001, determined once again to quit drinking at last. It was the first day of a new Millennium, after all, and seemed to call for a renewal of health and life. I felt like crap, of course, as most daily drinkers feel when arising. Not badly hung-over -- I wasn't, I tried to assure myself, like *those kinds* of drinkers. I was just vaguely headachy, a little sweaty, a bit sleep-deprived despite eight hours in bed marked by the usual restlessness and, as almost always happened, an awakening at 3 a.m. ("the drinker's hour") for a period of discomfort, rapid heartbeat and general self-disgust. I was 53 years old, deeply in debt and living alone after my second divorce.

But it was a new year! I knew where to turn for support! Things were going to change at last! I didn't even try to "spring" out of bed, but I slowly arose and, as always, stepped on the scale as my first foray into this brave new Twenty-First Century world. I weighed 290 pounds. That weight, with my height, qualified me as morbidly obese. My diet was egregiously bad, though perhaps not in the usual way for divorced late-middle-aged alcoholic men. I ate very little prepared food or restaurant food. Instead I cooked my own comfort food, heavy on meat, fats and quantity. Clearly, between my eating and drinking habits, I was killing myself and not as slowly as I might prefer. Intimations of mortality were becoming harder to ignore.

I was still a "functional" alcoholic. I was still able to run my bookstore, but my grip was slipping. And I wasn't even doing that well at many other aspects of life, such as romantic relationships. When my second marriage ended a few years previously, I learned, too late, that drinking and wise decisions about divorce don't go hand-in-hand. I agreed to a settlement that almost guaranteed there would be financial problems down the road for me. And, wouldn't you know, my business began a slow and seemingly inexorable downturn even before the final settlement, forcing me to sharpen my denial abilities and convince myself that the downturn was temporary. It wasn't temporary enough. Things didn't turn around until about the time I quit drinking -- what a coincidence!

That marriage had been rough, and I had felt that I had to end it to have any hope of quitting drinking. Smarter people than me knew enough to get the recovery process well underway before tackling the difficulties connected with a divorce. I reversed that formula and wasted several years in a fog as a result. I was 'functional,' but gradually becoming less so as one excuse for not quitting replaced another. Fat, drunk, alone, deeply in debt, a declining business, a declining life -- so many reasons to stop drinking. But they were the very reasons I gave myself for escaping my troubles through alcohol.

I had already proven to myself that 'support' is only one piece of the sobriety puzzle -- a vital piece, but not the only one. I woke up that New Year's Day in 2001 determined to try again. I had drifted away from the email group, feeling like I wasn't keeping up my end of the deal. I re-joined and I made a plan. It was for getting sober rather than staying sober (I'd worry about that when the time came). Most of all, it involved convincing myself that I had a future and that it didn't have to be a disastrous one. My divorce-related "maintenance" payments had finally come to an end with the New Year, so at least my financial situation wouldn't be getting even worse and I could let go of that excuse. In other words, my external situation was improved, making sobriety seem at least possible.

It still took me awhile, but the support from LifeRing was unwavering and after several months of more stalling, more failure, I made the leap. I won't say the rest was easy, exactly, but it was certainly much easier than I expected. It was foolish in the extreme to put off quitting for so long, but I had learned a very great deal since joining LifeRing two years earlier and once I jumped, I landed securely, always aware of the danger of relapse, but never doubting that my desire for sobriety was finally greater than my desire for escape from life.

Now, some 15 sober years later, I marvel at how much better my life is. Being a "functional addict" is certainly better in many ways than being a lost street-dweller searching endlessly for the next high. But it's only half a life, at best. The sense of wasted time (an especially apt phrase) is palpable, especially those two years after I found LifeRing but before I quit for good. My own experience taught me to be endlessly patient with others who struggle in their recovery. So often, people arrive at a support group enmeshed in difficulties that have to be dealt with on a daily basis. Problems with families, the law, money, mental health issues … "Recovery" means learning not only how to deal with things like cravings, but how to deal with the problems of life in some other way than getting drunk. It's easy to blame the addict for making lousy choices, but those choices bring results which are often well-established when recovery starts and dealing with those results can be a tough and unpleasant slog. Setbacks in early sobriety aren't inevitable at all, but to me they are totally understandable.

Quitting drinking was difficult for me, as it is for virtually all who reach out for help. Cravings that I couldn't resist; emotions that I desperately wanted to escape; resistance to learning the crucial elements of recovery ... all conspired to push success out of reach for way too long. But now I'm free of cravings, can deal with my still-difficult emotional life, and have learned what I needed, all without any "spiritual awakening" or reference to character flaws. No "higher power," no "God as we understood Him" and no "fearless moral inventory." Instead, LifeRing supported me when I needed it, taught me what I could accept and never, ever, told me there was something wrong with me. It was up to me to recover; LifeRing provided the patient, kind and tolerant help I needed. I will always be immensely grateful.

Story 4

Self-Empowered
by Adam Sledd

I walked into the large day room and sat near a group of guys around my own age. They were talking about their children. One by one, they related parts of their stories: how they came to be in rehab, often for the second or third time. Their legal situations, probation, parole, Drug Court. And, what really caught my attention: the various states of their parental rights and custody arrangements. Some had visits planned for the weekend. Others had social services involved. Some had significant others who were still actively using drugs and alcohol. Others had not seen their children in years … and were fighting to get the right to get to know them. Some had lost all or given up; it was too late.

It was 2011 and I had found myself in rehab for the second time. My own wife and son were home without me, again. I was faced with terrifying uncertainties: would my wife wait for me? Would I lose custody of my son? Would I be able to stay abstinent when I went home? Up to this point, I had been willing to pay the piper for twenty-seven years of heavy drug use. I paused … and realized it was time to stop.

My father had been an alcoholic. My parents divorced when I was eleven, and I experienced all of the trauma that came along with that. We had moved often, and I was the perennial "new kid." This combined with my selection for the gifted programs at school ensured my social awkwardness and targeting by the "cool" kids. In middle school, I found a group who would accept me; who accepted all the misfits. All you needed was long hair, an open flannel shirt over a t-shirt, and a chain on your wallet. I added a bandanna to complete the look; and I was home. All the mystique of my father's nights with the band, the little seeds that rolled out of his record album covers, the distinctive smell of the pipes on the rack in our basement … and rock-n-roll. It was exciting, romantic, and I finally felt like I belonged somewhere. It became my identity. And that is how I lived, for the rest of my childhood and the first half of my adult life.

My father's turbulent alcoholism left its mark, and I swore I would only smoke and never drink the way my father had. I finished high school, and somehow made it to college. It was a close call; by age 20 I was not only drinking but using drugs intravenously. Somehow, I managed to put the needle down, graduate college and work as a teacher for six years. I did a lot of things that, from the outside, made it appear I had my life together. But the reality was that I was a slave to drugs. My drug use was a prerequisite for any situation or relationship. No matter what else I was doing, I was using before, during and afterwards. I used, sold, and devoted myself to drugs. I went from one substance to another, trying to find the one perfect drug that I could use without consequence. It took years, but I slowly deteriorated, and the fun and excitement started to fade. It became a full-time job.

And then one day, I found myself facing felony drug charges. My son was a little over a year old, and I agreed to a Recovery Court program in order to avoid prison. It seemed like a no-brainer; I would simply fool them like I believed I had fooled everyone else up to that point. I served a nominal jail sentence, and they shipped me off to rehab. I was the model patient but was very skeptical of the 12-step programs that were being promoted as "the only way" to recover. Even though I was ambivalent about my commitment to recovery, I started asking the people who brought meetings in from the outside: "Do I have to believe in God? Do you know any atheists in the program?" I got a wide variety of answers; some gently nudging me in the direction of belief, some containing a bit of hope; but all were very cautious. It seemed that no one would really tell me the truth. This elusive, sometime tenuous relationship between secularism and the 12-step programs became a point of fascination for me and remains one to this day.

I went home, used again, and got caught, and it was in my second rehab that I realized how close I was to losing my son. When I heard the men in that room talking about their kids and their situations, it occurred to me that, at some point, they had chosen to keep using rather than raise their kids. The prospect of making such a choice horrified me, and I made up my mind then and there that I was through. That was the moment when my true self took over after 27 years of living through my addicted self.

Because of where I was and the resources that were available to me, I utilized AA. I figured that, even though I didn't fully subscribe to everything I was hearing, it would be a good foundation in recovery. When I got home, I switched to NA, which I found slightly more tolerant of my secular recovery inclinations. After a few years, I found myself struggling with the fundamentals of the program. I felt that secular people were under-represented and sometimes discouraged. After three years, I left the fellowship, taking with me the ominous warnings of those who dared not leave; and I have not looked back. I dealt with a good deal of inner conflict over those first few years; but it was my true self, my "sober self" that allowed me to navigate the 12-step program and make the changes I needed in order to stay in recovery. After years of living through my addicted mind, I knew all the hallmarks of my erroneous thinking and problem behavior. I was familiar with the lies I used to tell myself and willingly believe. What I recognized was that, for 27 years, I knew what was right. I had my true self with me the whole time. I was definitely susceptible to my heredity and the effects of drugs on my brain, but I also made a choice, every day, to live the way that I wanted to. I have heard people in recovery say, "Drugs never took anything away from me ... I gave it up willingly." And this was true for me. I was willing to pay the price, for a long time, until the price was unacceptable to me. At that moment, I made a different choice, which required some support and discipline at first; but which has grown much easier over time. I have not found it useful to live in constant self-doubt and superstition regarding my potential for relapse. The change is mine to make. I am constantly reminded of how I began making the change, and I work in many ways to maintain it. Recovery, for me, is regaining the power of choice and the ability to live confidently as myself.

I have stayed in abstinent recovery for over five years now and when I am asked how I do it, I usually say that I am simply trying to live a good life.. Some important parts of this are staying in tune with my feelings, working towards my goals, maintaining relationships with others, taking care of my physical and mental health, and altruistic service. Having a dogma-free, secular approach has made it possible for me to see the big picture of recovery and to get involved at so many levels. Being self-directed and empowered in my recovery allows me to hold myself accountable while taking satisfaction and credit for my accomplishments. I see myself as a whole, healthy person again and my illness is relegated to the past. I no longer have to live in the shadow of my addiction. I now work in the field of recovery support and I enjoy empowering others.

My son is now the main focus of my life. Taking care of him and providing a good life for us is the most rewarding thing I can imagine. Being a father has brought out all of the good things that were put into me as I grew up – the things that lay dormant in my addiction, waiting for me to return. I had everything I needed within me all along.

Story 5

The Conversation
by John Cutaia

He sat at the corner
of Blake and 17th downtown,
asked me for some change.
I pulled out a few quarters.

"Thank you, sir."

"You don't have call me 'sir.'
I'm just a person.
My name is John.
What's yours?"

"I go by Dell, D-E-L-L, like the computer."

He quickly launched into a story
about a woman who stopped and prayed for him
and right after that
someone gave him ten dollars.

Thoughts went through my mind about
correlation not implying causation
but all I said was, "I'm not religious."

"I'm not either, man,
but you got to have hope."

"I have hope," I replied
"and I'm not far from being
where you are right now."
"Most people don't talk to me.
I try to say something

and they just walk on by."

"People live in fear.
We're taught to live in fear."
"How come you're not afraid?"

"The most dangerous people
I've ever met
wear a suit and tie."

"I feel you," he said.

He wore a fairly new jacket
with some kind of sports logo on it,
his head and beard recently shaved.
He didn't smell. His clothes were clean.

"Where do you sleep at night?" I asked.
"In the shelter.
But they fill up early on cold nights."

"What do you do then?"

"I take the bus across town.
Then I take the bus back across town.
And sleep. Had a year pass.
But I lost it."

"You see that door across the street?" I asked.
"The one that says LifeRing on it?"
He looked but didn't seem to see it.
His dark brown eyes were coated
with the milky white blue of glaucoma.

"You ever been to a 12-step meeting?" I continued.
"Nope."

"Well, this ain't like that.
No praying. No God talk.
People just discuss what they're going through.
Gonna be a meeting there in a few minutes.
That's where I'm headed."

"Does it cost anything?"

"Nope. You can go in.
But if you've used today
they'll ask you to just listen
and talk to someone after the meeting."

"I smoked some crack this morning.
Right there."
He pointed across the street.
"I hate it. I hate myself.
I'm 51-years old and this is all I got."

"I know, man. I'm 53.
And I know how it is.
The drugs stop working
and all you do is get high
and think about your problems."

"I've tried to stop. But I can't.
I hate myself. Last night,
I was hanging out
with some homeless people
down at Five Points.
Someone asked
if I wanted to smoke some meth.
I had never smoked meth before."

"Yeah, how did that work out?"

"I hated it. I don't know why I do it"

"It's the same for everyone.
The part of our brain that stops us
gets damaged by the drugs
and we can't control it."
He stared down the street.
"I don't know -- I'm hungry.
I want to get me a burger.
They got burgers over there."

He pointed toward Lodo.

"Yeah." I said, letting that slide,
because I'm to the point
where I'm counting gas money.
Buying him a burger was not in the cards.
"I'm from Chicago." he said.
"I just want to take a bus home."

"Chicago is cold in the winter
and a storm is passing through right now."

"Yeah.
A bus ticket would be good, though,
or another bus pass."

"Look," I said.
"I need to go to that meeting
across the street."

I shook his hand.
It was rough as sandpaper
and strong.

"I'm going to hang out here

and pick up some change
and get me a burger."

I made eye contact.
"You're a human being.
You deserve a decent life."
And with that, we parted ways.

Story 6

Looking Back
by Tom Jarrell

There isn't anything remarkable about my story leading up to recovery. As a skinny kid with thick glasses and an eye that crossed, I discovered that alcohol was this magic elixir that made my shyness and concern about my looks go away. I joined the Navy just before my 18th birthday and by the time I got out at 21 my alcohol usage was well-established. I often say that the Navy taught me two things, electronics and drinking.

After I got out of the Navy, I moved from small town Pennsylvania to Denver, got a decent job and had an eye operation and got contact lenses, so my physical insecurity was corrected but my drinking pattern was entrenched. Like everyone else that I've talked to, alcohol served me for a brief time and then I served it for the next ten years.

Problems piled up quickly. I had a string of broken relationships and two DUIs eighteen months apart. I saw the same judge both times. He was not amused and sentenced me to 90 days in the county jail. Of course, I lost my job and found a lesser one when I got out, working for someone who drank as much as I did. Colorado had revoked my driver's license and told me that I could get it back when I could prove that I had been sober for a year.

I made a half-hearted effort. The woman that I was living with dragged me to an AA meeting and though my initial reaction was negative, after she moved out, I decided to give it a try. I learned a lot about alcoholism but didn't achieve any real sobriety. Next was a move back to Pennsylvania. I had determined that there was no reciprocity with Colorado, and I could get my driver's license reinstated there. I also decided that all my problems were in Denver so, with all that I had learned, I could find a way to make drinking work.

Of course, that was a resounding failure and what followed was the worst two years of my life. I tried to arrange my life so that I didn't have to drive. I chose an apartment that was close to my favorite bar and settled in. Blackouts were almost constant when I drank and that bothered me a lot. I tried to keep a journal so that I could note my thoughts when I got home at night and if I could reconstruct the evening the next morning it wouldn't be a blackout. If I could even read my handwriting, then what was on the page made no sense at all.

I was lonely and couldn't get a relationship going. In my early thirties I was hanging out in a bar populated by 50 and 60-year-old men. Even the bar owner suggested that I was someone who just shouldn't drink. I wasn't troublesome, I was just incoherent and fell down a lot.

I decided to just not drink. I had just acquired my third DUI and was afraid of more jail time, so I decided to just "white knuckle" it. That would work for about a week and then I would have to reward myself for being good. One Sunday night in a blackout I had an accident and had no idea of what happened. The following morning, I learned that a police cruiser had been side-swiped. My car bore the tell-tale signs of this collision. It really scared me, and I rashly decided to leave town again. For some reason, instead I called my brother and he took me to detox at the local hospital. I made arrangements to enter the inpatient program at White Deer Run, a very 12-step-oriented facility just south of where I lived.

Forty-two days later I was released and made arrangements to split an apartment with another recent inpatient from Deer Run. That worked. We immersed ourselves in meetings and kept each other going the rest of the time. I hadn't managed to make any friends that weren't problem drinkers since I moved to Pennsylvania, so I had to part company with my drinking friends. My new circle of friends became other people in recovery and that worked well.

It was strongly suggested that I avoid any drinking situations for the first year. I was willing to do that, but there was one major problem. At the time I repaired cash registers for a living. I talked it over with my boss and we decided that I would stick to the shop and he would bring in any bar register that needed to be repaired. That was cumbersome but it worked.

There were other stumbling blocks. I met the woman of my dreams. She was also in recovery, for even a shorter time than my one year. We moved in together and fought a lot. So with true alcoholic reasoning, we decided that we lacked commitment and got married. We really only had recovery in common and that couldn't sustain a marriage. After one of our many separations I packed up and moved back to Denver. She decided that she wanted to join me, so we went on for another two years. Even though we stayed sober, the marriage didn't last. I've now been married to a wonderful non-alcoholic woman for 35 years.

I had continued going to AA because it was the only game in town and I was committed to sobriety but was getting increasingly disenchanted with what I found there. I don't believe in god, so the higher power thing didn't work for me. At 12 years sober I was speaking at a friend's 10th year "birthday" and mentioned that I was involved in trying to start a secular group through the local Unitarian Universalist churches. The next speaker, who I knew well, ripped what I had to say up one side and down the other. At that point I thought "screw it", I have a good foundation in sobriety, and it isn't doing me or them any good for me to keep showing up at AA meetings. I detested the big book thumpers and even if I picked my meetings carefully, I couldn't always avoid them.

I was about to take a job transfer to Boston and when I got there, I just left the 12-step program behind. My one attendance at an AA meeting was when my newly sober sister-in-law visited around Christmas and wanted to go to a meeting. We found one and it was a big holiday group. The goodwill was strong, and I was thinking "you know, this really isn't so bad." Then a new girl spoke up and said the holidays were really bumming her out and one of the thumpers told her that if she was working her program, she wouldn't feel that way. Then I remembered.

I read about a new Secular Organizations for Sobriety group that was starting in Boston and became one of the founding members. It was then very similar to what LifeRing is now.

Ten years ago as I was celebrating my 30th sobriety anniversary back in Denver, I read that the Unitarian Universalist Association was starting an Addiction Ministry program which was to function as a referral service for members of the congregation who were trying to deal with alcohol or other substance abuse issues either personally or in their families. I became involved locally and, as part of my contribution, I was researching alternatives to 12-step programs. We also collected literature for AA, NA etc. I tried to find local SOS groups and from their web site got a list of contacts. It turned out that SOS had folded in Denver but one of the people on the list had become a LifeRing member. He gave me meeting information and that week I attended my first LifeRing meeting. Kirk D was convening, and I definitely liked what I saw. I've been a proud LifeRing member ever since. Kirk and Kathleen G were the people who really held it together in those early years. I still attend at least a meeting a week and act as a substitute convenor where needed. I'm also one of the contact people on our literature.

People need choices in their recovery. LifeRing fills a very strong need for many of us. I've got nothing against AA, as it has helped many people. For them a heartfelt thanks. But for the rest of us there are issues with that approach. It's too "one size fits all". I have problems with a higher power, powerlessness (except after the first drink) and I think that frequently sponsorship can lead to a very unhealthy relationship especially with very new people. Likewise, I'm so proud that LifeRing doesn't require a "hair shirt" of those who have failed and come back. There are others, but those are the big ones with me.

Some of the things that I've learned:
- Don't take shortcuts. Early sobriety is painful. If it was easy organizations like LifeRing wouldn't exist.
- Stay out of drinking situations early on. You probably don't belong in a bar just to socialize.
- If a friend's drinking is a problem to you, take a break from

them.

I'm a big believer in building a strong foundation early on. I function with non-addicted people every day and am just like them except for one thing. Alcohol doesn't work for me. There are many worse afflictions that I could have.

Go to meetings frequently. I still learn things after all these years. I sympathize with people just coming in, but it also serves to remind me of what it was like for me. I look at those two awful years that I spent at the end of my drinking as research.

I'm in my mid-seventies now. I date my sobriety back to the day I woke up in detox, December 2, 1974 so I observed 42 years of sobriety six months ago. If my health holds up, I look forward to celebrating 50 years in December of 2024.

Good luck to all of you

Story 7

I Guess I Had Seen Too Many Movies
by Anonymous

I loved the movies. Watching old movies on TV was an obsession. From Westerns to comedy to noir, they all had a romantic quality I could escape into. Of course, I wasn't conscious of the subtle conditioning that drinking alcohol was a mark of adulthood and urbane sophistication. Anyway, I would have rather been living large in a movie than my real little life.

I can see my 10-year-old self-leaning against our kitchen counter. Dressed in a cowboy hat and boots, a gun slung on my hip, I would sip or slug from my father's shot glass. Of course, the amber liquid in it was not whiskey. Apple juice would have to do. I wanted to be witty, bold, tough, suave, and grown up. Then I can see the fairly well-behaved adolescent finding some liberation in the tiny rebellion of smoking a cigarette with the girl next door. Drinking wasn't long after that. This won't be the autobiography of my drinking life. But some moments are worth mentioning.

After a long somewhat drama-filled romance with my first love I was thoroughly morose after she dumped me. I had grown sick of myself lying in bed and set about drowning my sorrows in drink. Easier said than done as I was still underage at the time. I borrowed my sisters ID and managed to get myself into my first bar. But not just any bar. In 1981 we called it a Women's Bar. It felt like home. It was exciting but safe. Here was a place I didn't have to lie about myself. I could be free. No shame here. Unlike the outside world, it was full of romantic possibilities, not to mention two-dollar pitchers of beer. So, I had my boldness with me too. There was laughter, joy, music, dancing and camaraderie. What a refuge it was.

When I turned 21 I got a job there checking IDs at the door. From that perspective I got to see how that refuge got sticky for some people. The old drunks repulsed me, and I imagined that in another five years or so I wouldn't be frequenting this sort of place in the same way. I had other things to do.

As it happened, those imaginings were far too vague. Five years turned into twenty. At some point in the excesses of the 80s I got myself to an AA meeting. This did not convince me sobriety was such a good idea. In fact, I really could not imagine myself as a nondrinker. But then it was only beer. And I was a connoisseur of it. My cigarettes were imported. I liked the illusion of control. I didn't have any dramatic consequences that I could see. No DUIs. No broken bones. I could delude myself this meant moderation. Mostly. Sober people were no fun. My identity was more easy-going bohemian. I saw healthy people as "other", across a growing divide. Yes, I knew smoking was bad for me, but I wasn't doing it for my health. More years went by.

Birthdays started to really bother me. My sober self-started to nag more loudly. Here I was over forty and still doing this? My unconscious plan to live fast and die young just hadn't quite worked out. I was as disgusted by myself as I had once been of my dad. I somehow found a sober mate thinking it might rub off on me. It didn't. The daily wind-down comfort ritual of smoke and drink in my back yard became the focus of my day. For a few minutes I could forget that I was unhappy. I had to strategize how I would get to that moment of comfortably numb. Every morning I would vow to myself I wouldn't make that stop at the corner store on my way home. And every day I let myself down. The daily betrayal left me feeling weaker and smaller. What was once convivial, and liberating had slowly become an isolating trap I couldn't see my way out of. I was half dead and wouldn't have minded if a stray bullet found me to finish me off. I was passively suicidal. I hated myself.

The heroic tale of me as protagonist in a movie had become a Greek tragedy.

I should say that all the while my misery was invisible to most people. I was not a falling down drunk. It seemed people with a more obvious problem would either quit or die. I detested the people who would always whine about quitting smoking after they had bummed a cigarette from me. As my dad used to say, "S**t or get off the pot!"

So as my sober self-worked on me toward deciding to get sober, that was invisible too. When it finally became clear to me that I might actually want to live, I started to strategize the how. How was I going to get past that corner store? What was I going to do with all that time I usually spent drinking? Was I going to have to check myself in someplace? I had decided long ago AA was not an option for me.

I started Googling and came up with LifeRing. I wasn't a big computer person, so I summoned the courage to go to a meeting. I wasn't sorry. No requirement to grovel or get down on my knees. No shame here, just listening. I found compassionate people with something in common, no matter how different from me in other ways. No awkward silence after I told my story. They gently encouraged me to try Kaiser, as I was already a member.

They assured me I wouldn't be forced to convert from my lack of faith to find it useful. They were right. I found a counselor I could talk to and talked about starting the program there. I had one interruption. My mother was deathly ill, and I had to travel home to help out. Old family habits die hard. I didn't make it back for a year. But a month after my 45th birthday I made it back to LifeRing and the Kaiser program. I give myself credit for my own research and strategy of what I needed. I knew I needed to be built up, not humbled.

So, here's some of what I learned…

Among the nuggets I got online from the old LifeRing Toolkit:

No one can get sober for you. Not your therapist. Not your sponsor. Not your rabbi. Not your pastor. Not your spouse. Not your fairy godmother. Only you can do this for yourself. Nobody else. So, don't wait for them to do it.

Treat yourself as though you are healing from an injury. Take time to heal. Don't expect normalcy.

Identify as a nondrinker. Drinking is not who you are.

There is more to belief than religion. There are many tiny unconscious things we have imprinted on ourselves that have to be brought to light and challenged. Little ideas or superstitions like "I can't do it", "It's too late", "She won't love me if she knows who I truly am", "No one cares about me." and BS like that. Self-sabotage can be sneaky.

Expectations lead to disappointments. You tell yourself stories all the time. What are they? Write new stories for yourself.

Pay attention to what you tell yourself. Be nice. Treat yourself with as much compassion as you would a small child. You may have to practice. You must love yourself enough to get sober. But it's certainly easier to love yourself when you are sober.

Rewire your brain. Take classes. Reconnect with your body.

I lost almost 20 pounds when I quit. There are lots of calories in booze. Dance, tai chi, boxing whatever! I dropped that story of "Other people are healthy, that's not who I am". Now I mostly do yoga and hiking. But dance classes and tai chi were a good start. The meditation class was the best. Listening to tapes on headphones was great too. Other people's positive voices in my head were somehow more believable than my own. When you are sober you can enjoy the world as you did as a kid. Be curious. Watch ants. Ride a bike. Play ball. There may be some aches and pains too. But life is obviously better without hangovers.

Don't get caught in other people's vortices. You have enough to worry about in healing yourself. Show up for people. Help others. Listen. That can be a very good thing. You have much to offer. But don't confuse which messes are yours to clean up and which are not. Remember that while no one can get sober for you, it works the other way too. You can't get someone else sober for them. They make their own choices and have to deal with their own consequences. Caring, compassion and boundaries all go together.

Find new comforts. You are not some unique kind of broken

because you became a drunk. Our culture encourages a quick fix. It's in every movie. Everyone wants to be comfortable. Everyone avoids pain and discomfort, in a million ways. But everyone suffers sometime. Self-care is learned. Recognize when you are avoiding something and be curious about it. It doesn't have to be a problem. Being uncomfortable doesn't mean you have to do anything about it. Patience takes practice. Find what makes you feel good aside from ingesting things. Nature works for most people. Mindfulness, Meditation, or exercise for others. (See notes on the senses.) Now I can find refuge in my own breath.

Nothing lasts forever, especially feelings. Fear isn't very useful. But you don't have to chase it out of the room when it comes to visit. Be grateful. It's an attitude. Forgive yourself. Life may not be fair. Things do not always go according to plan. Change what you can. Accept what you can't. Pay attention. You have at least five senses. Use them all. After years of numbing it can be invigorating to take in scents and tastes without filters.

Get to know your feelings. Know those feelings won't kill you. Sometimes we automatically think something feels bad, when it's really just unfamiliar. Elation is something to savor not dampen. There can even be a richness in grief. Feeling alive may be foreign at first, but you are going to love it.

If you live with integrity, you will live shame free. Be honest and authentic. Not just with others but especially with yourself. You will be amazed how much energy you free up but not having to sneak and worry. Poetry and beauty can save your life. For me it was Mary Oliver's poem Wild Geese. Look for what resonates for you. Choose happiness.

Honor your sober self. It's the true nature you were born with. Confidence builds every time you face an obstacle and let the sober you take the reins. Perceptions become more reliable. I remember my joys now. I have also been present for and dealt with so many challenges in the eight years since I quit smoking and drinking it feels like I have slayed dragons: Divorce. Injury. Diagnosis of a terrible disease. Debt. Depression. Death and grief...

I wrote a new script. I earned my liberation. I chose life. I found love again. I can still be hard on myself. Life isn't perfect, but maybe I'm that hero after all. And maybe even a little badass. You can too. Believe that. Make a plan. You are stronger than you think you are. Be a badass. Live. A huge thank you to all my LifeRing pals for all your listening and support.

Story 8

It's Never Too Late to Get a Life
by Nancy Corbett

I got very drunk the first time I tried liquor: it made me sick and I got into a fight. There was a clue, but I wasn't paying attention. The old saying that life is lived forward but understood backward was true for me. Alcohol created problems for me for years before I understood its role in the drama.

I was born in southern Ontario, where liquor sales were strictly regulated until the 1970s. You had to be 21 and have a permit to buy alcohol and your purchases were all recorded; the clerk could refuse to sell you liquor if he thought you were buying excessive amounts. As teenagers, my friends and I raided the supplies of our parents or paid compliant adults to get a bottle for us.

Neither of my parents were problem drinkers. We didn't have wine with meals and a cocktail was something exotic like something in a novel. Throughout my teens and later, at university in Vancouver, I had some narrow escapes from risky situations when I drank, but my drinking was restricted to parties and other social occasions. I certainly drank far too much at times and did things while intoxicated that were disgusting and/or dangerous, but alcohol was not part of my daily life.

It was when I moved to Sydney, Australia in 1974 that things changed dramatically. It was commonplace for people where I worked to go to the pub at lunchtime and after work, especially on Thursdays (payday) and Fridays, the start of the weekend. Because I was an alcoholic - although I didn't know it then - having a drink or three in the middle of the day flipped the switch in my metabolism that demanded that I drink more, more, more. There were times I couldn't remember getting home from the pub after work.

I started buying alcohol, hiding it under the kitchen sink at home and drinking before I went out to events. If people were coming over, I bought much more than was required and drank most or all of the excess. People were surprised at how drunk I seemed after a couple of glasses of wine, unaware of the half bottle of vodka I'd consumed before. I began to have the personality changes and irrational behavior associated with the progress of alcohol addiction. People around me were worried. I was worried too, especially when I started having blackouts. It was frightening when hours and even entire evenings were simply erased from my memory as though they hadn't happened. Sometimes I woke up in the morning, or came to, on the floor. The fear and remorse that accompanies alcoholic drinking became constant.

It got worse. I began taking various pills to numb myself, to mask hangovers, to quell panic attacks. I know now that I was severely depressed but then, I didn't understand what I was dealing with. I had virtually no sexual feelings, or feelings of any kind, except I was prone to both irritation and apathy. When I drank, I felt relief for a short time, followed by despair and anger.

By the middle of 1974 the drinking binges had become so frequent, and my behavior so reckless, that something had to change. Everyone close to me was frightened and hurt and although I didn't care very much what happened to me, I cared about them.

I went to my first Alcoholics Anonymous meeting in July of that year. It was a relief to discover that there were lots of people who reacted to alcohol as I did and to realize I wasn't insane in spite of my compulsion to drink even knowing it was destroying me. I left the meeting feeling hopeful. Recognizing the problem meant I could address it. If drinking made me crazy – and it did – all I had to do was stop.

I had no idea.

I didn't know then how many alcoholics struggle all their lives with this addiction, and that many of us never achieve any lasting recovery, no matter how hard we try or how strong our desire to free ourselves. I didn't know that there's no cure, only remission, and that remission depends on many factors, not just self-control. I never saw myself as a powerless victim, but I had to learn the limits of my will in dealing with my addiction to alcohol.

I met some great people in the AA meetings. They were sharing similarities in their stories, particularly in terms of their inability to control their drinking once they started as well as the ways in which alcohol changed their personalities. I identified completely. I went to a Sunday afternoon meeting that had a membership of actors, comedians and writers who were quick to tell me that the notion of creativity being enhanced by alcohol or drugs was a myth. I knew that liquor sometimes seemed to help my writing flow, but the creativity was within me, not the bottle. I had to find other ways to engage creatively. Alcohol may lessen inhibitions, but only temporarily.

As I learned more about alcoholism, many of my unacknowledged memories began to surface. I'd been hiding some frightening truths from myself for a long time and I couldn't do it any longer. A lot of confusing things started to make sense when I looked at them through the lens provided by recovery.

After two months free from alcohol, I got drunk again. But this time, I hadn't wanted to. This time, I realized staying sober wasn't simply a matter of willpower. This time, the consequences were worse than before. Any pleasure I'd gotten from drinking in the past, or even relief, had vanished. Now it was just sickness, fear and despair.

I made a determined effort to get my mind on the 12 Steps of AA and make them work for me. I had no trouble accepting the second part of the first step, admitting that my life was unmanageable, but accepting that I was powerless over alcohol went against a very deep belief that I was NOT powerless, and that I was responsible for what I did. As an activist and feminist, it seemed wrong to voluntarily adopt a doctrine of powerlessness, and when I tried to argue myself into it, I failed.

I had trouble with the following two steps as well, which required a belief that God could restore me to sanity. I didn't believe

I was insane and while I was sure that the universe contained many immense powers, all of them unimaginably weightier than my temporary and limited existence, I was unable to conceive of a personal God, though I tried. I tried to do what I was told, to "fake it until I make it" but although I was pretty good at fooling myself, I never managed that.

In the following years I had periods of freedom from alcohol that lasted a few months and even, once, for three years. During each sober stretch, my life improved immeasurably, and every relapse felt like a huge failure. Finally, in 1990, I got sober and stayed that way until 2004. I went to AA meetings in Australia (which is a much more secular country than the United States, and generally practices greater tolerance in its AA meetings) and in various other countries during my travels.

I don't think there's a single cause of alcoholism. To me it has always seemed more a matter of genetic predisposition + unresolved trauma + ready availability of alcohol + social acceptance + pressure to drink + early feelings of relief when drinking = alcoholism.

When I relapsed by drinking wine at the party to celebrate my 60th birthday in 2004, I was horrified. Months passed before I drank again. But I had opened the door, and gradually I began drinking sporadically, then more regularly, and then almost daily.

When my partner and I retired and moved to Tasmania in 2010, I went to the local AA meetings and found myself unable to engage with them at all. Fortunately, by then I'd connected with LifeRing.

I sent for the LifeRing Recovery by Choice Workbook and Empowering Your Sober Self and became a daily reader of the LifeRing emails and forum. Through them I developed real friendships with some other members, who supported and encouraged me through a number of relapses and setbacks until I finally got some traction in 2012.

I've now been free from alcohol for two years and 10 months, with the help of Antabuse, the unfailing love and honesty of my partner, and the assistance of people in LifeRing. They never judged me, but they also didn't sugar-coat their concern. I needed all the help I could get to achieve sobriety again, and I found that help in LifeRing. I am more grateful for that than I can say.

Recovery is an ongoing process, and so is my commitment to LifeRing. I need it to remind me to keep my priorities right, and I love being part of the recovery process of other people. This is the toughest and best thing most of us will ever do.

Story 9

Badassery
by Dennis Meeks

When I tell non-runners that I run marathons, the first question I get is "Why"? And, it's a very good question.

I have always been running from something, most of us have, I think. Now I am running toward something: sobriety. But unfortunately, I have to run through a ton of bullshit to get to the other side. And I need help to get there.

At the tender age of 63, after finally (hopefully) getting off the crazy-go-round of serial relapses that had been ongoing for 3 years, I decided I would run six marathons in six months. The first two or three went well, so I upped it to 12. But then I thought, "What if I get injured and need some time off?", so I added one more, #13, so just in case I had to skip one, I could still finish 12 in 12 months.

Running, now I am speaking literally - feet pounding the pavement running - and getting sober are not that that dissimilar. I've been running on and off for decades, but for the last several years, especially 2010 through 2013, my literal running was more off than on. I started training again in July 2013 after quitting drink and drugs on June 29. Some may think it borders on masochism to train for one marathon, and just plain craziness to train and run one every month for a year. But, not so fast. I had been drinking myself senseless with alcohol for years, so why not run myself sober? I needed a goal to strengthen my sober resolve.

Running became my "go-to" therapy: running, hurting, growing and getting stronger with every training run and my self-confidence dimly reflected in the sweat of my contorted face at the finish line of every marathon. It's difficult to drink (like I drink when I drink) and exceed at anything other than failure and regret. Running was helping me change all that.

So, my first marathon time this year was a 4:23, not bad for the aged among us. I was stoked. And six months later, I had a personal best at 4:22. And I kept going. Running. Not drinking. Repeat. I ran in the rain, sleet, and the heat of the Tennessee summer, when I came to understand the splendid relief that shade trees and sobriety offer. I ran when I didn't want to run, I ran when my feet hurt, when my calves cramped, when all I could do is put one foot in front of the other. I ran when I didn't like myself and have kept running now that I have discovered that, hey, I'm not so bad after all. I'm stronger, tougher, more disciplined than I thought. I have endured. By god, that's what I do, I endure.

Marathons are hard. Thirteen in 12 months is harder. I ran on beastly hills, I ran in the ugly parts of strange towns, and I ran in the glorious Utah Canyon in Provo. I ran a marathon that was stopped because of an impending ice storm in Little Rock AR (I was at mile 18 – I wasn't going to stop because of a little inclement weather - and finished anyway with an official time.) I ran in Tupelo MS on the last day of August where the heat is oppressive and humidity worse (like running with a hot blanket wrapped around your head.) I ran a midnight marathon in rain-soaked darkness that consisted of running five boring times around a five-mile loop, and then 1.2 miles to make it an official marathon distance. I ran the Flying Monkey Marathon in Nashville in November, in a forest of hardwoods the color of copper with swaths of still green foliage providing a peaceful patina over a course with 7,200 feet of total course elevation change, up and down, up and down.

And, finally, I ran in the desert at the Tucson Marathon. I could have been on the moon, the landscape so different, yet breathtaking, from that which I am familiar. The only forests there consist of cacti and shrubs. I plodded, I lumbered, I shuffled, but I always finished. Every freaking one of them. I fucking endured.

And I have been sober every day of this marathon year. Again, not that much difference between running marathons and staying sober. Both are stinking hard (marathons literally so), insanely challenging, and infinitely rewarding. However, although running is a superfluous gift, abstinence is essential. Moving forward, letting go, looking back without going back, friending sometimes without being befriended. Falling down, getting up, getting it wrong and making it right.

My first days sober were much more frightening (and more important) than my first trip to the marathon starting line. Running and sobriety are exhilarating, generally, while drinking is always, without exception, a dead end for me. Smack, thud, every goddamned time.

Now, I run "somewhere" because I am determined not to drink "anywhere" anymore. I run because the physicality of it makes me appreciate what I have and what I almost lost. Running and sobriety prepare me for what's ahead. I had begun to wonder how many more times I would see the sun rise, the moon slide across the night sky, experience the explosive delight of a thunderstorm, hear my 14-year-old daughter's infectious laugh, or feel my wife's embrace. I started thinking about being 63 and actually did some math….and it was sobering, no pun intended.

Now, I see more days ahead. More active, sober days. When the alarm screams in my ear in the morning, I awake reluctantly, but gratefully without a hangover or owing anyone an apology.

Then I toe the starting line of a new sober day, game face on, experienced, excited and still a bit frightened of what may come.

But, hey, I'm a total badass. Bring it on.

(Special thanks to LifeRing and the friends I have made there. Without their support my marathon year would never have happened)

Story 10

Powerlessness
by Philip Henderson

Two dead mice
One fresh, one slowly desiccating. Its head chewed eyeless.
A new lock on the dingy door and new keys.
Inside the wooden floor was covered in something dark, like tar.
A chair upended.
Bottles, more bottles, one open, musty smell.
An expensive wine glass with some wine left.
Is the glass half empty, or half full, or twice as big as it needs to be?
I smile at my obsessive thinking and gently pour the wine outside
the door.
The mice are still there
A final symbolic act, closure? control at last. If only…
Trust Her to use an expensive glass for her last drink.
I look closer, wedding present.
Shit.
A heaviness in my chest. I looked at her chair where she was found
lifeless.
I sit
Guilt and sorrow. I tried to help but had to go. This was no way to
die, alone.
Bottles, bottles and more bottles. Powerlessness.
When did she die? We don't know…
The when doesn't matter
The loneliness does…

Story 11

Magic Has to Happen Somehow
by Bobbi Campbell

At a LifeRing Annual Meeting I attended a few years ago, it started off with everyone in the room going around and sharing what we'd learned about ourselves in sobriety that we didn't know before. Despite the many important and valuable things, I've learned about myself and life I never knew until sobriety, when it was my turn, I said the first that thing that came to me. "I'm not a piece of shit."

Yes, really.

*****

As it happens, even though part of my story of recovery is inextricably linked to AA, and while it was an almost entirely negative experience for me, I didn't become involved with secular recovery because I'm an atheist, or because I'm constitutionally incapable of being honest with myself or others, or any particular set of reasons or philosophies, or whatever. The bottom line is that I wanted to be sober more than I wanted to keep drinking, and as you know, that's not a place one comes to quickly or easily.

I'd known I had a problem for a long time, depending upon how well I was or wasn't able to keep the secret from myself. When Caroline Knapp was doing the press tour for her book Drinking: A Love Story, published in 1996, a magazine interviewer asked her how someone could tell whether or not they were an alcoholic, and her answer sent paroxysmal shivers down my spine: "If you think you have a problem, then you probably do."

I was only 24 then and convinced myself that if there was a real reason, I didn't have my drinking together it was simply because I was doing it wrong. If I had any hopes and dreams of getting through the rest of my life successfully at all, then I would just have to learn how to do it right.

As things tend to go, life didn't get better for me. I had managed to hang on to a great job in healthcare that I was pretty good at (even though on any number of different occasions they could've – and probably should have - canned my ass). I also maintained a close relationship with my mother, some family members, and a few friends who I never saw because that would've required me to do something else besides stay home and drink. And my love life? It was strangulated by alcohol, alcohol, and more alcohol. But eventually another part of me started to pipe up, started to interfere, started growing scared and weary of waking up every morning, so sick and ashamed of what I'd done to myself, again the night before. I was so afraid someone else would find out what was going on that I did everything I could to prevent it: lying my ass off to anyone within my immediate radius, myself included; desperately hiding everything I could from everyone else; making up as many excuses for my behavior as possible; and above all, isolating myself. It helped if I believed I didn't really need people that much, anyway.

Whatever I told myself – I'm not going to drink tonight. OK, I'm only going to drink two beers tonight. OK, fuck it, I'll drink tonight and then start sobriety over again tomorrow - there was always a Scylla and Charybdis component to my drinking, a siren song that kept me smashing myself up on the same rock over and over, again, and again, and again.

But there was another part of me wouldn't shut up, either, so by the end whatever relief or enjoyment I still got out of drinking lasted for about 10 minutes. Then I'd spend the rest of the night crying my eyes out, until I passed out.

I've come to understand that the only people who get what I wanted out of a drink are the ones who don't have a problem with it, but I stayed stuck in that schizophrenic loop for years. At some point I had what is known as a "moment of clarity" in which I realized for the first time that I was not put this planet to live and die a sad, lonely, pathetic drunk – no one is. Furthermore, I was wasting whatever I had to offer the world by not becoming who I am meant to be. I didn't know who that was, but I wanted to find out.

It may have been a year or more after that when I finally stopped drinking, it may have been a few weeks. The way time had escaped me, it's hard to say. Then in 2007 I got a computer, and it changed my life.

*****

Eventually I came to the conclusion that despite my best efforts over the years – and I tried; boy, did I try - I wasn't going to be able to do it alone, so the first item in the order of business was figuring out where I could get some help that wasn't AA or 12-step-oriented (because I'd tried that, too). I assume you've tried that – finding something not 12-step oriented. Not that easy, is it?

At the time, a search of the web yielded enough results that I finally stumbled upon something called LifeRing. I was very excited about the prospect of going to a different kind of support program. I related to the concept of the Addicted Self versus the Sober Self that I read about on their website, because that's exactly what I'd been dealing with for years – the constant battle between one and the other, the addict running roughshod over everything, and the other part of me that desperately wanted it to stop. I loved the idea that I had a Sober Self who could prevail.

I learned after a thorough perusal of the LifeRing website that there were no face-to-face meetings in my town or anywhere near my town, but they did have a nice online support system in place. I thought, "What the hell, give it a try. If I don't like it, I'll try something else."

In the LifeRing online community, I found a nice group of clean and sober people, as well as others like myself: people who were newly sober and scared half to death, who didn't understand how a message board could be of any practical use, but willing to give it a go. It had a great batch of current posts and threads going as well as a handy, easily accessible archive of messages that one could read through when no one else was around to talk to.

Once I got up the courage to start posting there, the first thing that struck me quite plainly was something someone there said to me, a wonderful woman named Margit. I had started my own thread on the board and said that I just wanted "it" — the horrific addicted part of myself making its hideous, incessant demands that I continue drinking, the consequences be damned — to go away and leave me the hell alone!

"It's not going to go away from you," she replied. "You have to go away from it." Something about that just clicked with me, and I had my first real clue of how this thing was going to work: No magic fairy was going to come along, wave a wand over me, and release me from my prison. The good news was, it was up to me. The bad news was, it was up to me. So, I was going to have to be my own magic fairy. (I had more in common with Broom-Hilda than Glenda the Good Witch, but OK, fine, whatever I had to do, I'd do it).

The first thing I did was give myself permission to go in whatever direction felt right to me in my gut – something else I'd long ignored - and that's how I found one of the LifeRing email groups.

I had no idea what the hell an e-mail group was, much less how it could help me with my sobriety, but the description of this group on the LifeRing website appealed to me right away: "An email list for those seeking Support, Affirmation, Friendship and Encouragement (S.A.F.E.). It's a strong, secure place where we seek to nurture the 'sober self' that exists inside us all."

So, I joined. Craig, the list's moderator, sent out a requisite "Welcome" post introducing me, and I received a few warm welcome posts from other members. And then I waited, watching other emails coming in and how it worked. Everyone seemed really nice, and I responded a few times to a few different people very, very tentatively, and mostly just read all the messages as they came in. But nothing really happened to me on my side of the screen. So, I waited some more, still trying to figure out the right time to jump in. And then, after being sober for a couple of weeks or so, I relapsed. Again.

And then, the dam burst. I'd had it up to here, and I sent out my first real post to the group, a treatise, if you will, on why I was there, and that I needed help, but I was scared to death that I couldn't be helped, and what the hell was wrong with me, anyway?

It was like a revelation when other people in the group, particularly those who had significant sobriety, took the time to respond to me and tell me about their own experiences. They were so kind, so open, thoughtful, embracing. I felt more accepted, included, cared for, and respected in this group than I had with any other group anywhere ever before. I learned it was safe for me to tell them the truth; who I'd been, and what I was going through, because I had to – I had to be the one to engage.

In return I received plain, practical talk about what my Addicted Self was doing versus what my Sober Self could be doing, along with a whole lot of encouragement.

I chose to believe them when they told me it would get better (it did), when they said all I had to worry about right then was staying sober (it was), when they not only told me this thing was possible, but that I would do it (because I could)! It was especially great to connect with other people all hanging on to and helping to steer the same little life raft – you become like a band of sober Spartans, fighting back the turbulent sea that threatens to take all of you under – and when you feel like you've actually been of some use to others in some way, whoa. There's no better feeling in the world.

You see, much to my surprise, I discovered that I, the Patron Saint of the Perpetually Lonely and Insane, too, needed people. Just like everyone else does. I may not need them in droves, but I saw that I could not only make friends — and I've made some wonderful, wonderful friends through LifeRing — but I could also shore up someone else who needed it in real and meaningful ways.

****

By this point you might be thinking, "Soooo…am I to understand that this person, Broom- Hilda or whatever her name is, got sober online?" And perhaps you find yourself feeling a tad dubious, because that's not really something you've heard of anybody doing, right? It may seem impossible, but there's something very special about allowing oneself to be vulnerable with other people, and to hold one another gently, even over great distances through satellite hookups and fiber optic cables (although it's all wireless and Blue Tooth now). It was certainly the first time in my life I'd ever participated in anything like it, but that's how I did it, and it saved my life.

For the first several months I ate, drank, slept, and breathed sobriety via the list. I checked in with it while I guzzled my coffee first thing in the morning, I posted many times throughout the day, I read posts and wrote my own in the evenings, and checking the list was the last thing I did before I went to sleep at night.

******

Writing is how I best express myself. Always has been, but I didn't understand just how much I'm able to purge myself of whatever it is I've been holding in or reinforce ideas enough to realize they apply to me, until I started emailing the group. It made things...real for me.

One of the things I've come to understand is just how much my reality is very closely tied to my perceptions and beliefs about things, the result being that in many, many ways we really do create our own realities. In other words, we are what we believe. Really, it's that simple – whatever we believe we are at a core level, that is who we are, and we find out what these beliefs are by questioning them.

In this way, I could begin differentiating my addictive voice from the voice of my Sober Self, and then isolating the voice of my addictive self so that I no longer had any meaningful attachment to it. I was able to identify when my Addictive Self would begin "romancing the drink," conjuring up sodden old images of how beautiful my drinking life had been, like in those commercials. Yep, good times with good friends, lounging on a white sand beach together...basking in the glorious sunshine of our lives...

After a while I could also quickly devise a snappy comeback to any of its subversive little suggestions. Here's a brief example of a typical inner of dialogue:

It: "Oh, wouldn't a nice, cold drink really be wonderful right about now?" **Insert wistful sigh of longing here.**

Me: "Oh, yeah, a drink's a great idea! So, would sticking my hand in a blender and hitting frappe!"

It: **Insert the sound of a needle being ripped across a record, and then…crickets here.**

Me: Yeah, that's what I thought, ya jackass.

Eventually it also gets so you can hear someone else's addictive voice coming out into the open, too. It always exposes itself one way or another, a lot like a serial killer might, making the hairs on the back of your neck stand up. I also learned to distract myself with something else while "It" would natter away, and before I knew it, "It" had shut the hell up and I was on to better things. Either way, I learned two things: This, too, shall pass, and I have the patience to wait out whatever "this" is. The only way out of anything is through it, such as a feeling, for example. I learned to not only feel my feelings, especially the negative ones, but also not to do something to avoid feeling them in some way. To just…sit with them. To go from one moment to the next, taking each moment, and each feeling, as they come.

I started to get the hang of a few other essentials, like don't take the first drink. A second at a time, a minute at a time, an hour at a time. Twenty-four hours at a time. Lather, rinse, repeat. Like taking it easy instead of allowing myself to become overwhelmed by the enormity of just how much my drinking had fucked my life over six ways from Sunday. Like making sobriety the number one priority in my life and making all of my decisions based on it. The journey of a thousand miles begins with a single step and all that. If these concepts sound remarkably simple, well, it's because they are. But simple doesn't mean easy.

My sobriety date is November 28th, so my first month in was during the holidays but it really didn't bother me all that much. Even through hanging out with my brandy swilling, beer chasing family that month, I didn't care about it anymore than I had to – I didn't even put a tree up that year - and it all went just fine. In years past, to me the mere idea of trying to quit drinking during a holiday – any holiday - would be like trying to smell the number 9, so getting through that was huge for me. I was really, truly doing this thing!

*****

As it turned out, I learned more in the first six months of sobriety than I had in the entire 35 years prior, stuff I honestly never knew about life that most people probably know by the time they're five-years old. To begin with, I didn't know that I had any intrinsic value. I believed that whatever I had to offer other people or that I was good at was the result of luck or happenstance. I had no idea how self-esteem is built; I always thought people just attained self-esteem, and then they had the confidence to go out and do whatever they wanted to do. Not so. Action begets action, stasis begets stasis. Newton's Laws apply to more than just minute particles or apples. Life is action: You do stuff, then you gain self-esteem. Who knew? Oh, right - most five-year-old …

Remember that old story you always heard when you were a kid about how when you fall off a horse you have to get right back on it again? Yeah, that shit's true. It's not that you fall – everyone does; you are not defective because you did. It's whether you get back up. And getting up doesn't mean that what happened to you doesn't matter or that your pain isn't real and shouldn't be acknowledged. In fact, you may need to give yourself a little time before you put your foot in the stirrup again. The point is, to get to the good stuff you have to scrape yourself up off the sidewalk, get back in the saddle, and start over again, even though it's scary. Otherwise, how are you going to know what you're missing?

Eleanor Roosevelt once said, "You must do the thing you think you cannot do," and that became a mantra of mine, because I didn't know I had the capacity to learn new things the same way everyone else does. Really. I thought that my not being perfect right out of the gate, and my inability to learn some things as quickly as others, were indications of basic incapability on my part. Persistence, a quality I do possess in spades, is my major ally in almost all things, and as long as I persist in trying, and failing, and getting back up and trying again, without allowing myself to cave to the recurring feeling that I am doomed, I end up being alright.

It's taken me a while to process that, on a fundamental level, there's actually nothing wrong with me, when I believed there was everything wrong with me. When I got sober, I had to learn how to trust myself in a way I never believed I could. More than that, I learned to stop being so afraid of everything all the time.

So, I took the ball and ran with it. I gave myself permission to try new things, to try, to fail, and then to try again. As a result, I've experienced more joy, more awe, more gratitude, and the best times of my life since I got sober. I joined a public speaking organization. I took a writing class. Went out with friends. Grew closer to my family. Best of all, I met and married the love of my life, Rich, a fellow LifeRinger whom I got to know through the Safe list and email correspondence, at first as a good friend. Our friendship eventually grew into more, much to my surprise (I still can't believe it sometimes), and thanks to him, the door to an amazing life was flung wide open.

I learned to swim, then to snorkel, and then to scuba dive. I mean, shit – scuba diving? I thought that was something only extremely capable individuals like Jacques Cousteau or the dudes on "Wildlife Kingdom" did. Never in my wildest dreams did I consider myself someone who would ever attempt to swim in the ocean, much less go down into it and look at all the unimaginable beauty beneath. I've traveled the world to places I never thought I'd ever see in this lifetime. I moved from my old hometown – which I thought I'd never leave – to the huge metropolitan area where my husband made his home, and I enjoy all kinds of fun things we do here together.

I have also experienced the deepest sorrow, loss, grief, and depression of my life since I got sober, too. My Mom – my beloved Mimsy, as I call her - became ill with cancer, and I spent the last year of her life caring for her as well as I could, which at the time didn't feel nearly good enough, and still doesn't. Watching her die broke my heart; so did spending another year saying goodbye to the home

I grew up in, and everything else about her I couldn't save. In the middle of all of it, my brother, another fellow traveler on the sober highway, iterated a very simple, guiding principle that saw me through then, and still does now. "You don't have to drink. You just don't." Neither of us did, and I'm so grateful for us both.

I have my darling Rich to thank for introducing me to so many incredible things and fostering them in me, and for being my biggest support and best friend in the worst of times. I also have sobriety to thank for all of it.

*****

As time's gone on, I've come to think of myself as a work in progress. For the most part I use a lot of the same tools as I did in the beginning because many of them are just as relevant now as they were then. I've spent time away from my support group as well as time with it, and time with it is always better. I have no problem with the concepts of being in recovery and recovering, and that I'll need to stay grounded in and connected to it, for the duration of my life – that's just how it works for me, and I'm fine with that.

But things have evolved over time, too, and I've begun to do deeper work on some of the issues that have followed me around and that I hadn't been able to do as a younger person. There's this thing called balance, that two different things can both exist and be true at the same time, and you can learn to negotiate between them. And now I'm finally trying things I've heard about but never really done before, like meditation, cognitive behavioral therapy, and psychotherapy. Trying to make use of the time I have as means to the best ends. To figure out what I want to be when I grow up! To be who I was always supposed to be, and a huge part of that is accepting myself the way I am.

*****

So, there you have it – how I learned and grew exponentially into the sober giant you see before you. Recovery has given my life meaning. Seriously, I had no life to speak of prior to recovery, and I wouldn't have one without it now. One of the major ways I remain in touch with and participate in my recovery is by volunteering my time to LifeRing. For a while it involved doing some writing and social media work, but who knows how things will evolve in the future? Maybe I'll even bite the bullet and start a face-to-face meeting!

I still find myself fascinated about the true nature of whatever addiction really is, and how the human mind works, because I think for the most part we still don't really know, which makes it that much harder to treat things like addiction. The brain is a largely undiscovered territory, and being a human being is complex.

More than anything, I want everyone who wants recovery to have it, and that might mean that one thing or another may not work for you. If I can tell you anything else, it's just this: Please don't condemn yourself if something you've given your best effort to doesn't work for you— you're not a failure, and you're not alone. A secular approach to recovery worked for me; it might work for you, too. If not, that's OK – keep looking and trying until you find what does work for you. You – the real you – are worth it. Your life is worth it.

Story 12

I Am Not an Alcoholic!
by Catherine Henley

Hi, my name is Catherine, and I am not an alcoholic!

Yes! I have struggled with a serious alcohol addiction for 35+ years, but there is no way I am going to call myself an alcoholic today. Why?

Because an alcoholic …

can't stop drinking for even one day

has to drink in the morning; otherwise she gets "the shakes"

hides the vodka bottles from her family and drinks in secret

can't walk past a liquor store without going in and buying a bottle (or more)

goes on "benders" for days and can't remember what she did

has a disease that makes her drink more and more

"hits bottom", loses her job, and all her money

ends up in jail, in the gutter, or … dead

Before I quit drinking, I had known for a while that I had a problem with alcohol. Too many times I experienced not being able stop drinking. Sometimes I was not able to remember what happened the night before and when reminded I would cringe in embarrassment. It was not unusual for me to wake up on a Saturday or Sunday morning with a terrible hangover and need to spend the whole day in bed to recover.

And there were those times when I drove my car while under the influence of alcohol, even when I had my young son in the car. I remember one Sunday late afternoon, on my way home from a family Easter gathering, I pulled to the side of the road to get more wine from the cooler. From the back seat my observant ten-year-old son said "Mom, you don't need any more wine." Thankfully I was sober enough to agree with him and for the next hour drove home in a shocked stupor.

Even though I didn't think I was "that bad," in my late 30s I quit drinking alcohol because I didn't want my addiction to negatively affect my ability to be a good mom. I was a single parent who worked hard to provide a quality life for my son (his Dad lived on the other side of the country).

I began my sober journey attending Alcoholics Anonymous meetings. I had previously picked up The Big Book when I acknowledged I was struggling with a pretty serious issue with alcohol. Some of the stories in the book rang true, some were very old-fashioned, some, even comical! But I did not relate to those stories as they described experiences that were much worse than anything I had ever encountered.

From that reading, I learned all about alcoholics and alcoholism. I learned that if I was really an alcoholic, I had a serious and severe disease and that, if I didn't stop drinking, all the shocking stories that I heard and read would happen to me, if they hadn't happened already.

This did not sit well with me, because my life experiences so far were nothing like these stories. I did not drink every day, and my life, overall, was only getting better (or so I thought.) I was advancing in my career and my finances were improving. My friends said they didn't see me as having a real problem with alcohol and some were surprised, even offended, that I stopped drinking.

Knowing in my heart I had a problem with alcohol, I continued my sober path and made the commitment to "work the program." I was encouraged to go to "30 meetings in 30 days" which was not an easy task as I was a single mom, but I tried to attend as many meetings as I could.

There was something comforting about being in a room of people who were dealing with the same controlling and painful issues I was. I appreciated the opportunity to be honest with myself as I spoke out loud when sharing my story. I was grateful to receive the AA chips -and subsequent hand-clapping - as I passed each milestone.

I enjoyed going to "Speaker Meetings," as some of the stories people shared were quite interesting! Although I would usually say to myself, "Wow, I'm sure glad that never happened to me!"

I found a sponsor and picked up the Twelve Steps and Twelve Traditions reference book. I started "working the steps". It was a challenge for me to work even The First Step: "We admitted we were powerless over alcohol - that our lives had become unmanageable."

Admitting being powerless already sounded defeating to me, and my life was certainly not unmanageable.

But I had to admit that I had more power over my life without alcohol so after working the first step, my sponsor agreed I was ready to go on to The Second Step:

"Came to believe that a Power greater than ourselves could restore us to sanity."

As I was raised agnostic, this was a difficult concept for me to accept. I was not imprinted with a religion and had very few religious influences. My mother was raised Catholic but left the church before she met my father (who was not religious.) As a child, the times I had to go to church with my Italian grandmother, who was a dedicated Catholic, were difficult for me as the atmosphere was so serious and ominous.

As a teenager I had a very negative reaction to the word "God." I detested the idea that some man up in the sky was watching all my moves and judging me. As most of the people in AA referred to "a Power greater than ourselves", as God it was hard for me to get past my prejudice. Fortunately, as time went on some of the AA members suggested I create my own version of a "Higher Power" and this did help me.

So, it was on to The Third Step:

Made a decision to turn our will and our lives over to the care of God as we understood Him.

As you can probably imagine, due to my prejudice about the word "God" and the idea that "God" was a "Him", I resisted the idea of making a decision to turn my will and my life over to the care of God as I understood Him. To help me move through it, I was reminded again to replace the word "God" with "Higher Power." But I could not get past the "Him" part. This is when I heard from some of the AA members to "Take what you can and leave the rest". They were acknowledging that the AA program may not be a perfect fit for all people, especially those of us who are not religious.

As difficult as it was for me to ignore the references to God and to my being "powerless," I diligently worked through the rest of the twelve steps with my sponsor. I tried to take what I could and leave the rest. When I struggled, I replaced the words "Him," "His," or "God" with "My Higher Power".

If I mentioned to anyone in AA that I didn't relate to most of the stories in the books, and what I heard in "the rooms," they gently reminded me how fortunate I was to have made it to AA before my addiction got any worse. I was told I was a binge drinker or a high bottom drunk, and that no matter what, I would hit the same low bottom that other people had experienced if I "went out" (left the AA Program). I used to say, "I wish there was an 'AA Lite Program' for people like me."

After achieving two and a half years of sobriety, I was not convinced I was an alcoholic. I could not associate myself with what I perceived of alcoholism, so I stopped going to AA meetings and slowly allowed myself to drink alcohol again. Everything was okay, for a while.

Over the next 15 years, after experiencing numerous appalling events, and traumatizing family members or myself due to drinking too much alcohol; I tried to quit several more times on my own without attending AA meetings. I was able to stay sober a year here and there, but always fell back into the mindset that my addiction to alcohol was manageable.

After yet another harrowing experience, I quit drinking again by enrolling in an outpatient treatment program for six months (my health insurance paid for most of it.) I really appreciated this program as it provided information on addiction from the medical perspective, which I did not receive in AA. I was educated on brain chemistry and what happens to the brain when one drinks or takes drugs. They emphasized the importance of one's individual relationship with their "substance of choice", encouraging us to review all aspects in our lives that may be contributing to that relationship.

I learned that my tendency to overdo it with alcohol was multi-leveled and complex. Not only do I have a predisposition for alcohol abuse from both sides of my family, I also suffer with depression and mood swings. It was reassuring to learn that there were some genetic and medical components that contributed to my inability to "Just Say No".

At the conclusion of the outpatient program, they encouraged us to attend AA meetings to stay sober. Knowing it was helpful to have people to support me and relate to, I anticipated attending AA meetings with the hope I could benefit without having to invest myself fully in the AA program.

I went to an AA meeting on my lunch hour from work. I was shocked to hear the attendees still reassuring themselves with all the sayings I'd heard before, many of which I found demeaning ("Keep it Simple, Stupid" is one example). "Wow," I thought to myself, "is this what I get to look forward to? I'd rather be a "functioning alcoholic" than attend these meetings for the rest of my life!"

It was very depressing for me. The AA scene was just not my style. I was disappointed that members didn't like you there unless you were dedicated to getting a sponsor and working the steps. For me, there were too many rules to follow (or stumble over) causing me to feel negative about myself. I was saddened as I continued to hear the fearful warnings of awful things to come if I drank again.

Yet here it was, fifteen years since I last attended the program, and my life was yet to be in the gutter! It just made no sense to me and placed me in that same familiar position of questioning "my alcoholism."

Then there was the religious reference. At the end of a meeting, as we got up to hold hands and recite The Lord's Prayer, I left.

Even with all my newfound knowledge on addiction, I only stayed sober for a year and a half. In a weak moment, I allowed denial to take over once again and convinced myself that I could manage drinking alcohol. I struggled with my addiction for several more years. I didn't lose my job (although I found out later that my production level had been at an all-time low.) I didn't end up in the gutter, but inside, my "Sober Self" created conflicting emotions forever reminding me that I was a very unhealthy and unhappy person.

Ultimately, a little over five years ago, I was arrested for driving under the influence. My blood alcohol content was .19. I guess I hadn't needed that last shot of tequila before leaving. The whole experience was extremely disturbing for me, and was, finally, "my bottom." When I got home from those two days in jail, I was convinced: I can no longer drink alcohol. I have to say, this was the most difficult conclusion I have ever come to in my whole life, I felt like I was cutting my arm off.

Knowing if I were to successfully quit drinking alcohol I would need some kind of support, I did some internet research and found LifeRing.

LifeRing appealed to me right away. It was the first time I had seen another program or philosophy that supported recovery from addiction that was not a 12-step approach. In fact, I found out there were other people out there, like me, for whom AA just wasn't the right fit. I was elated!

As there were no face-to-face meetings in my town, I got my support online. I am a "techie" by profession so spending lots of time on a computer was normal for me. I joined all the LifeRing online support groups and really appreciated the honest input I got from the members who shared their stories and provided me with guidance.

I picked up the book Empowering Your Sober Self by LifeRing co-founder Martin Nicolaus. It was life-changing. The LifeRing "Three S" philosophy of Sobriety, Secularity and Self-Help completely resonated with me. I was grateful that I did not have to turn it over, but instead, I could empower myself with knowledge of addiction – MY addiction - and develop wisdom to help guide me to live without alcohol regardless of my personal religious preference or spiritual belief.

The philosophy I was taught from LifeRing helped me to own my addiction. It makes more sense to me that in recovery we have to rely, not on a "Higher Power," but on ourselves, and our ability to stay sober, by using the helpful tools and philosophy we pick up along our sober journey; pertaining to our own personal story of addiction.

A few years ago I had the opportunity to represent LifeRing at the annual meeting of CAADAC (California Association of Alcoholism and Drug Abuse Counselors.) This was such an enlightening experience for me! I was grateful to represent an alternative to 12-step programs and most of the people I talked to had never heard of the secular recovery support program options such as LifeRing, Women for Sobriety, Rational Recovery, SOS or SMART Recovery. Many agreed that the 12-step approach is not for everyone who deals with addiction, but there was hesitance to the idea that "an addict" could be in charge of their own recovery program.

Looking back, I can see that the AA program and working the steps have been significant parts of my spiritual path in recovery. They helped me to accept and appreciate a "Power greater than myself," something I prefer to call "The Universal Oneness." I also learned to have faith that what comes next in life will be okay, and that I can't control everything.

At the same time, the benefits that I have gained from LifeRing to stay sober are profound and long lasting. I am finally convinced, once and for all, that I can no longer drink alcohol. This internal conviction is based on knowledge rather than on fear. It is based on my power, not another power. I appreciate the trust that I am allowed, and the belief that I can manage my own life. And that just because I have been battling severe addiction does not mean I am weak or immoral.

Now that I no longer suppress uncomfortable feelings with alcohol, I can move through them and get to the other side of understanding why I am feeling these feelings. Having the ability to reflect on my feelings has helped me to change my own negative behaviors, which were unwittingly contributing to my overall anguish. This could only happen once I stopped drinking.

I don't call myself an alcoholic. This label carries negative images and feelings for so many people. Why should I bring up negative connotations that are painful? If asked why I don't drink alcohol, I say, "I choose not to due to my physical chemistry."

This truth resonates with me, and I don't have to feel bad, in fact I never have to feel bad again. I'm learning how to feel good by facing, owning and moving through my personal issues – vs. burying them with alcohol and wallowing in my anxiety.

I feel truly empowered. Thank you LifeRing!

LOVE/PEACE to All

Story 13

Friendship
by D.L.H.

Growing up in a big, highly religious family, I did not think I would ever drink. Drinking was bad. It was a sin. In fact, the first time I ever tasted alcohol - in the form of beer at a high school keg party – I found it to be disgusting. Much later when I discovered wine, I knew I had found a friend.

It started out innocently enough. Wine made socializing so much easier for an introvert like me. It also made most dinners taste better. There were even health related claims touting that red wine was full of antioxidants that were good for our hearts. So going to wine tastings in search of the perfect, super-dry red became my passion. I loved it whenever I found a bold red wine that was so dry I could hardly believe it was liquid as it slid across my tongue. Palisade, Napa, Sonoma and the Willamette Valley were all on my frequent travel list to visit wineries.

Then somewhere along the way – not exactly sure when or how it happened – the case price at my local liquor stores became much more appealing to me than finding that one great bottle of wine. Why bother with going to the vineyard or the wine tasting, I thought, when all this perfectly acceptable wine was just around every corner in my neighborhood. Like many functional drinkers, I rotated my purchases around a half dozen or so liquor stores to prevent them from thinking I might be drinking too much.

During this phase of my life, I had a really good-paying job, which I enjoyed very much. It involved about 75 percent travel and working from home the balance of the time. While this was a wonderful freedom, at the same time it was also quite problematic. I had started switching between straight vodka by day and red wine by night. It became routine for me to join conference calls, make phone calls, accept incoming calls and write email responses while drinking and working from my home office. When I traveled, the company I worked for paid a car service to take me to the airport and to pick me up when I got back. This meant I could drink before leaving home, and I often drank at the departure airport, on the plane, sometimes at the arrival airport and later at the hotel where I stayed. My job required travel to other workplaces to solve problems, yet I sometimes had to drink a little in the morning to prevent arriving with shaky hands. Other days I just suffered through the after-effects of drinking heavily the day and night before. On one occasion I missed a flight at a regional airport because I did not allow enough time to check in at the ticket counter having grown accustomed to the speed of electronic ticketing which that small airport did not yet offer. That flight was easily rescheduled although I had the inconvenience of spending most of the day there without access to alcohol.

It seemed I was able to maintain the basic job expectations for a long time. I was even asked to go to Hawaii once to handle a situation that the person assigned to that location could not seem to remedy. At any rate, my performance slipped because my focus was on when and where I'd find the next drink, even though I really thought I was doing a good job of concealing my daily drinking habit.

My first realization that I was not actually hiding this excessive drinking as well as I thought, came when my boss suggested I take a lateral position in another state. There was never any discussion about drinking being the issue or perhaps me needing a medical accommodation. I was told I had not developed strong enough relationships with site leaders and because of that, my performance was below expectations for my current role. I did not confess to having a drinking problem nor did I ask for any accommodation, though in hindsight that could have been a better potential solution for me. I declined the offer to transfer to a lateral position in a different state because I had family in the city where I had been living. This meant I lost that job.

All of this made it obvious to me that my drinking had become a problem for others. So I phone interviewed psychiatrists who specialized in treating addiction. Based on my strict religious upbringing which led me to an aversion to all things god-like, the primary condition was to find someone who would not tell me to go to Alcoholics Anonymous. I had read enough about 12-Step meetings to know that the constant references to God or another higher power would not work for me. The shrink I settled on had assured me that I would not have to go to AA. He used a daily gradual reduction of drinking approach to wean me off alcohol over a one month period. Once I was sober he said, "You gotta go to AA now." So he lied to me initially. Anyway, I really tried to make AA work and was actually successful at it for six months.

After that I thought, I got this, now I can just "manage" my drinking. It worked marginally well for about three years. I was lucky through this period of time to avoid potential legal consequences with my car. One summer day I took my car to the shop for some transmission work. I did not realize ahead of time that it would take several hours to complete. The mechanic said I could walk to the Starbucks at the end of the block to wait, so I did. When I got there, I noticed that there was a liquor store two doors down that would be opening soon. I got a cup of coffee and drank some of it. As soon as the liquor store opened, I bought a 500 ml bottle of vodka and dumped the rest of the coffee out to pour vodka into my coffee cup because I was sitting outside. I sat in the sun and alternated between reading, drinking and phone activity. By the time my car was ready, I had finished the bottle and walked back to the auto shop. I thought everything was fine. I paid the bill and was waiting for them to pull my car around. The manager came out and very politely said that he was going to have his mechanic drive me home in my car. I did not live far from the shop but clearly, I had overindulged just in the time it took them to fix my car. That auto shop manager could have just as easily called the cops, but I got a pass that day.

Another time on a summer night I drove downtown to drink. I remember wanting to have a few martinis at a restaurant/bar known for the way they make their martinis. I had already been drinking at home part of the day. When I got to that restaurant bar I parked on the east side of the street. I went inside and ordered a straight up,

Stoli, slightly dirty, dry martini with an extra olive. The bartender brought my drink with a glass of water that I had not requested. When I finished the first drink I asked for another, but the bartender said she had to refuse serving me another, asking instead if I'd like to order some food or have some coffee and sit a while. I was highly offended, so I paid the bill and got in my car and drove a few blocks north to another bar. This time I parked on the west side of the street. I walked in, careful to be sure to put on my best sober look and ordered the same martini. They served me there…and served me another one after that. When I decided to go home I went outside looking for my car. My drunken memory failed me as I was certain I'd parked it on the east side of the street - the side I parked on at the first bar – not on the west side, where I parked at the second bar. I walked up and down the same two blocks at least 20 times and could not find my car. I happened to be wearing heeled sandals that night and my feet hurt so bad I sat down on the strip of lawn between the sidewalk and the street to take my shoes off. I was afraid I must have accidentally parked in a tow zone and not noticed the sign. A man approached me and started talking to me. He said I could not sit there, at least not for very long. He told me I could get arrested for public intoxication. I thought I was so normal, and I had never heard of anyone getting arrested just for being outside, not driving or bothering anyone. Finally, I called a cab to take me home thinking I'd worry about my car the next day.

When the next day rolled around, I had to call another cab to take me down to the scene of the assumed tow away zone, thinking I would find the phone number to call the impound lot. I remember being very embarrassed telling the cab driver that I lost my car. He said it was not uncommon. He had picked up other people who needed help finding their cars. I thought that was insane, but have to admit that somehow, it made me feel a little bit better. When we got to the block where I had parked, he asked me what kind of car I had. I described it, and very soon after that, he said, "Is that one it?" as he casually pointed to my car on the west side of the same street where I had searched in vain the night before.

Oh, the façade of normalcy that active addiction makes us

believe we are living!

I rode the roller coaster of self-deception, with all its sober ups and drunken downs, until the day I chose to drive my then three-year-old grandson home from my house in a big city to his house in the country. He had spent a three day weekend with me, and I had consciously avoided drinking most of that time. However, Monday came, and mid-morning I asked him to help put some of his things back in his little suitcase so we could get going. Being a three-year-old, he took everything that was already in the suitcase out instead. It seemed like it was going to take a long time before we left, so I started drinking vodka straight from the freezer. Then before we got on the highway, I stopped at a drive up liquor store to get more vodka. The drive up was conveniently located right next to the McDonald's drive through where I bought a chicken nugget happy meal for my grandson. We started the one hour and fifteen minute drive to get to his home. When we were a block away from his house, he saw the dollar store sign from the back seat and said, "Grandma, Grandma, I want a toy."

If I had been sober, I would never have indulged him. Instead, I would have reminded him of what a lucky little boy he was to already have so many toys. But since I was drunk, I stopped, and we went inside. That was when my blackout drinking episode came to an end, as I lost consciousness and collapsed to the floor.

I have been told that my brave, young grandson walked over to the store clerk pointing and saying something like, "Look...my grandma fall down". This tiny country town has under 2,500 residents and had only one police car at the time. Once it was determined that I had no immediate life threatening medical condition, I was cuffed and placed in the back seat of that police car. Fortunately, for my grandson, he got a fun ride around the block with the emergency crew on the town fire truck. Then I was arrested and taken to the county jail where I stayed for four days. Even though I was not driving the car at the time, I was later charged with DUI and child abuse.

The aftermath of this event was life changing for me in many ways. I considered treatment programs but rejected most of them because of their focus and insistence on the 12-Step approach as the crux of the cure. I recalled wanting to drink many times after leaving those meetings that I had attended regularly for six months years ago. The treatment programs I viewed as possibly being viable options were not covered by, or did not accept, my insurance. I guess it could be said that the many consequences that ensued served as my initial treatment. Those ramifications included numerous legal proceedings, random drug testing, 26 sessions of drug/alcohol education classes, community service, and most significantly, an Interlock device in my car for two years.

The less tangible and truly more important outcomes include constant work to rebuild a fractured relationship with my son and daughter-in-law. After all, I could have put an end to their handsome, vibrant and smart child's life on that perilous day. The facts of how close I got to that possibility are not lost on me. Further, getting and staying sober required a sensible, reality based plan. Being able to create my own sobriety and recovery plan without the influence of religion has worked for me. Traditional 12-Step programs did not work for me because of the religious based requirement to surrender my free will to some mysterious power that I could not ever believe in.

Through all of this I learned that wine/alcohol never really was my friend, although I certainly gave it many chances by going back to it over and over again. At best and for short time periods, it provided a false sense of confidence and security. Yet some parts of my life seem to be a blur because of it. I am so happy I was able to find a group that supports people who pursue sobriety through secular and self-directed methods. Now I recognize my real friend as LifeRing Secular Recovery. Lucky for me and other like -minded people, all the many friends I have made there come along with it.

Story 14

My Recovery Story
by Mary Lee Peterson

I got sober on June 9, 2009, at the age of 62, after six years of progressively heavier and heavier drinking.

My father was an alcoholic and committed suicide at the age of 39 (I was 18 months old then). It was a big family secret, but I knew that drinking was an evil to be avoided. My mother's family had an intolerance to alcohol which probably explained why it took so little alcohol to put me under the table. Between the time I was 18 and 53, I probably got drunk less than a dozen times. My habit was to have maybe one glass of wine when I went out to dinner, approximately once a month.

Then in 2003 I lost my job. Suddenly, I had lots of time on my hands and a severe blow to my pride as a highly useful and valuable employee. I began to spend evenings out on my patio, and gradually my drinking became daily, and then daily to stumbling oblivion.

While I didn't go out to drink, I did a lot of drunk dialing (and if I called any of you, I apologize because I don't remember whom I called or what I said). Starting in 2007 I began to see a therapist and began to tell her I was concerned about my drinking. In 2008 I planned a trip to my niece's home, and I realized I couldn't get drunk every night while there, so I stopped. I had no problem not drinking for three weeks, but the day I returned home, I got drunk and drank just as I had before I left home.

In late May 2009, I woke up one morning and said to myself that I wasn't going to drink that day. At 5:00 p.m. I was on the patio drinking. I was shocked, so the next day I said the same thing, "I won't drink today." By 5:00 p.m. I was out on the patio drinking. I have always thought of myself as a woman of my word. When I choose to do something, I follow through. My self-image was shattered! The next Thursday, I was at my therapist's office and told her that I couldn't quit, and I was scared. She asked me if I wanted to stop. I said yes. She got up from her desk, went to the phone, made a call and handed me the receiver. It was the Kaiser Chemical Dependency Recovery Program (CDRP). I made an appointment for the following day, went in for an interview and signed up for the following Monday.

So now what to do about the alcohol in my refrigerator? Friday night I followed my usual pattern. Saturday, I tried to finish everything up because I had decided that I wanted to be 24 hours sober before starting my program at Kaiser. I couldn't finish it all and I left it in my refrigerator for a couple of weeks and was not tempted to drink it. I threw away all my wine glasses because I thought they would be a trigger.

My CDRP was 12 weeks every day, all day. I learned so much and found so many new friends. I found LifeRing the first week in recovery at the Kaiser facility. I went to a few AA meetings, including one called Godless Heathens in Oakland, CA. I liked the group but was unable to do even the first step. I found it disempowering to think of myself as powerless. I hold that I am totally powerful over alcohol – unfortunately (or fortunately?) the first sip is the only one I can say no to, and I know that deeply and firmly.

I had a few situations in which I was tempted to drink and a few situations that I avoided in early sobriety. I now take my own favorite soda to every gathering so that I have what I love to drink. When at a restaurant and the waitress asks, what do I want to drink, I never say I don't drink but instead I ask if they have raspberry or any other kind of lemonade.

Ever since I was six months sober, I have convened one or two LifeRing meetings per week. I am so grateful that LifeRing exists, and every meeting reminds me of where I never want to go again, as well as where it is possible to still grow. I am grateful for the opportunity to 'give back.'

Story 15

Magical Mystery Tour
by Richard Campbell

The hardest thing about telling my story is knowing where to start. I guess I'll start with some dates and numbers, as they've become rather fascinating to me.

Summer 1965: almost exactly 50 years ago, I drank (and got drunk) for the first time. That would mean I was 13.

April 1985: I went through my second rehab and began my longest period of sobriety.

March 1995: I picked up a drink and blew that ten years of sobriety.

June 2000: I discovered SOS, and later that summer became a member of one of the LifeRing email groups. That, of course, was almost exactly 19 years ago.

February 2010: I had my last drink or drug

What is it with me and these multiples of five? I have no idea, but here's the rest of the story:

I'll try to make this part quick, but my story isn't complete without my early years of drinking and drugging.

Okay, back to the summer of '65, as I got drunk for the first time with my buddy Mike. We raided my Dad's liquor cabinet and began mixing up various hideous concoctions ("suicides," as we aptly called them) and forcing them down.

The number one singles on the charts that summer have all become iconic 60's anthems now, from the Byrd's cover of Dylan's "Mr. Tambourine Man" to the Beatles' "Help" to the Stones "(I can't get no) Satisfaction" to Barry McGuire's apocalyptic "Eve of Destruction." I can picture all of them as apt background music for my first bender. In fact, a line from "Mr. Tambourine Man" could be considered my motto for much of my life thereafter:

"Let me forget about today until tomorrow."

In retrospect, the not-so-amazing thing about the first time, and all my early drinking experiences, is that they were the same as all my later drinking experiences; I drank, liked the feeling, and then wanted another-and- another-and-another until I was very drunk.

I came by my alcoholism rather honestly, it would seem, in that Dad was a horrendous drunk. In terms of the nature/nurture debate, I guess I've got both bases covered, in that he was also verbally and physically abusive, so I had a pretty traumatic childhood.

I was introduced to pot in '67, and for a few years my friends and I turned up our noses at alcohol, terming it "a limited high." But I did end up smoking "non-habit forming" marijuana nearly every single day for about the next fifteen years. In about 1970, while living in a dorm at USC, I was busy turning people onto pot, but I had one friend who insisted I drink some beers with him one night, and I discovered that they blended rather nicely.

Throughout the seventies I was your basic party animal. If you had it, I tried it. My first addiction that worried me was that I was a speed freak and gobbled up "whites" every day in large doses. I also estimate I dropped acid over 200 times, and all of this was accompanied by copious amounts of alcohol and marijuana.

I never had a moderate phase of drinking. I was the guy, pretty much every night, who wanted to make that last run to the store, for more. I hung out with friends most nights, and although my group included some other hard drinkers, I was the one that wives and girlfriends didn't want to see come over, because it inevitably meant a late night.

In the late 70's, I added cocaine to the mix. How I managed to drag myself to work after some of these all-nighters, I don't know. I know there were any number of times I hadn't even been to bed and had to attempt to hold my breath every time I passed someone in the hallway. Some mornings I even brought vodka and added it to my coffee. It helped to be young, and it helped that I was working in the family business, and it helped a LOT that I was in sales, and so could exit the building after making my token appearance in the morning. Sometimes I went home and went back to bed, and sometimes I actually went out and did my job. I did well enough, despite all the partying, that I began to make some big contributions, and move up in the company. By the late 70's, I was in effect running things while my dad was in his other office, the bar down the street.

I had my first child in 1982, at the age of 30, and by the summer of '84, when I first went to rehab, had another on the way. I had acquired much more work responsibility, as in the midst of my parent's divorce, my mom, brother, and I forced my dad out due to drunken belligerent behavior, and I was made acting CEO. It was weighing on me that I had helped remove my Dad, due to his alcoholism, but that I had my own unaddressed problem. Suffice to say that we needed armed guards to remove my dad from the building, and needed them around for quite a while afterward, after numerous episodes of violence, death threats, et cetera.

Something in me knew I needed help, if I was ever going to be a responsible father to my kids and manage a small business with around fifty employees. I do remember, however, sobbing uncontrollably on my way to my first rehab, thinking that my life was basically over.

On the evening of my second son's birth, in January 1985, I relapsed, taking advantage of his mom being in the hospital. I went back to rehab in April, after an intervention.

In both of my rehabs, I was given the standard "go to AA" prescription, and I complied. I was also forced to confront my unhappy childhood, and the fact that I really had no clue about this thing called "feelings."

I struggled with the whole God concept in A.A., but I did as I was told and began to make some wonderful friends. I am grateful for those ten years, as they enabled me to be a sober dad during my kid's most formative years, and also gave me a chance to come into my own as a businessman. To some extent, I'm still living off my success during those years.

The biggest mistake I ever made, I think, was that when I began to question a lot of AA's dogma, I also questioned the notion that "once an alcoholic, always an alcoholic." Surely, I told myself, all this intensive therapy I've had over the last ten years, has enabled me to "grow," and I'm not the same man I was when I first quit ten years ago. I had done a lot of maturing, true enough, and had dealt intensively with my childhood issues.

Nevertheless, I had basically no success in becoming a moderate drinker and didn't really even try very hard. My downfall is I became a "just this once" drinker, which was as much an illusion as moderation.

I had split up with my kids' mom back in 1988 and met someone in 1996 (during a wet period) who, I can now see, was something of an enabler. We decided to get married, and I decided I should sober up for about six months prior to our wedding in 1997, but we had always planned to drink at our all-inclusive resort in Fiji (I mean, come on, they were giving out bubbly French poison).

When I told my best man (my best friend from AA) about this plan, he calmly told me "that's the stupidest thing I've ever heard," and stepped aside. I plugged another AA guy into the role, but of course I did drink on the honeymoon, sprained my ankle drunk-dancing, and all but ruined the trip.

I tried, here and there, to get sober again, with some success, but seemingly could not make it over six months. My wife had once said to me, "I don't see the problem in having a blow-out every quarter or so," and boy did I like the sound of that. The problem was, it ended up being more like every two weeks, most of the time, and I was combining the drinking with prescription diet pills, which rather mimicked the amphetamines I had taken in the 70's.

An article in the L.A. Times, in June of 2000, featured an interview with a psychologist, who talked about alternatives to AA. What? Where? I got the guy's number and called him, and he told me about SOS. I started attending, and started to acquire some new tools for sobriety, such as the Sobriety Priority. They also told me "Do Not Drink No Matter What," which I thought was kind of stupid, at first. I mean, yeah, but how? More on that later.

I also picked up a copy of a book they had on sale, called Keepers, and some reference was made to the source of these gems--an email group which was hosted by Tom S. I knew nothing about how such lists worked, but I signed up, and tentatively began participating. I still thought this was connected to SOS, but I eventually figured out that LifeRing had splintered off from SOS, and the list was part of something called LifeRing.

I was enamored, from the outset, by the concept of communicating with a bunch of articulate and like-minded sobriety-seekers, from all over, and immersed myself in the list. I was sober for about six months, but in early 2001 I went off on a ski trip and decided to dip my toe back in the poison waters. I then wrote a post to the list confessing my relapse and tried to point out some ways I was minimizing the harm. This didn't go over well, to say the least. In those days, the list was prone to very heated discussions on all manner of topics, which sometimes devolved into what can only be called flame wars, and I found myself in the middle of one. I announced a quit date about a week ahead of when I wrote, and took some heat about delaying it, but that increased my determination to stick with the quit date, and I did.

Thus began my longest stint of sobriety in LSR, prior to my present nine plus years. For the first time since relapsing in 1995, I achieved a year, and then two, and then seven months beyond that. Of course, just as in my prior decade of continuous sobriety, I got a lot accomplished. I had been having some difficulties with my eldest son, but we got those resolved before he graduated from high school and went off to Brown. Two years later, my youngest also graduated, and went off on a free ride to college, which was good news to my bank account. I started a new business, which continues to the present day. I have somehow been able to generate a decent income without working long hours, allowing time for other things---like travel.

Jump forward to September of 2003: I'm on the deck of a cruise ship, leaving Ft. Lauderdale harbor, and they're handing out free drinks. I decide to take one, and I remember earnestly telling my wife that sobriety had become my default state, and that I would resume as soon as we returned home. The somewhat sad thing is that I fully believed it. I know you're shocked, shocked, Dear Reader, to hear it didn't work out that way---not even close, as I continued to drink off and on the remainder of 2003, and on through 2004 as well. So, my one week vacation from sobriety turned into 17 months of intermittent bingeing.

My LSRmail friends were supportive, for the most part, although as time passed I had a sense, probably not inaccurate, that folks were losing patience with me. Finally, in February of 2005, I got it together again. I had a one-day relapse in November of that year, but rather amazingly got back on the horse and rode it until late in 2007.

I should mention that I had taken up racquetball back in the mid-eighties when I first got sober, and it had become a passion. I started developing knee problems in the mid-nineties, and in 2007 had my second useless (studies have now shown) torn meniscus repair, so I did have some pain when we embarked on a big European adventure later that year. I had some hydrocodone pills, which my wife held, and I really did try to be honest about whether I needed them or not, but for me there are always fine lines, and I wonder whether I might have trespassed slightly during that trip.

I gave them up after our return, but I still had ongoing pain. One night, while web-browsing, I happened upon an advertisement for some sort of knee pain clinical trial. There was a questionnaire, which I filled out, and I was then told that I qualified. I was directed to call some number and sign up. In the fine print, I was told more about the study, and it emerged that an investigational medication was going to be administered, but that the control group would not be given a placebo, but, rather, oxycodone. I knew about oxycodone, and in fact it was a big part of my first relapse in LifeRing, as I had gotten hold of some Percocet from a Canadian doc, while on that ski trip.

Anyway, back to the clinical trial. I recognized it as a hazard and decided against pursuing it, but I didn't tell anyone about it either. I almost forgot about it, but a seed was planted, and my addicted self cultivated it in secret for a month or so, until it sprouted, and I signed up for the thing.

This required that I go to a doctor's office about 20 miles away and get fully evaluated. Once I was approved, I was given some nondescript gray capsules, with instructions as to how to take them. I remember I took the first one on a Saturday, and afterwards it seemed to me that I had never felt so good in my life. It didn't take me long to pry open one of these large gray capsules, where I found two small round pills residing, which a little googling revealed were each 20 mg of Oxycontin, which I had heard about but never tried.

Of course, I had not informed my wife that I might be taking oxycodone and wasn't about to tell her now. I took to waiting until she went to bed at around 9 PM, and then I'd crush them on my desk and snort them, something else I learned about online.

I managed to not drink for a month or so, but of course my resolve was rather weakened by my secret drugging. The clinic, by the way, kept increasing my dose every few weeks, so I started getting bonus pills. I had to keep a "pain diary," and show up at their office weekly, which I willingly did, although never once did I feel as good as I did that first day. I was caught in the old "chasing the first high" thing I'd always heard about with heroin addicts. I wanted that peaceful floaty feeling I had that first day, when the world was good, but I never quite got there again. Of course as time went by I was taking more and more, and I knew this was going to end badly. It did, when the gal at the clinic suddenly told me that the study was over, and I'd receive no more medicine.

After making rather a scene, I was able to persuade the doc to prescribe me 30 more 20 mg pills, but by then my daily dose was 100 mg. Needless to say, I went through withdrawal, despite trying to taper.

Around then I came clean to the Safe List, and to my wife. I asked her, at one point, whether she had noticed a difference in me while I was doing all these drugs, and her response was kind of classic: "I just thought you were getting stupider."

So, around April of '08, I managed to wean myself off Oxycontin. It was tough, and I remember thinking that I would never feel happy again, but I got through it.

This saga may have had something to do with what happened later that year, when my wife suddenly announced that she wanted a separation. It emerged that she had taken an interest in another guy. Thus began a very difficult challenge for my sobriety, in that she was still living with me, but spending every evening with the dude, before coming back to sleep here.

It isn't as though all was perfect in our marriage, but I had not considered ending it, and was shocked and hurt that she had decided to do so. She had her problems; for starters, she was a hoarder, and if you've seen the show Hoarders, you know what large parts of our house looked like. She was also chronically late for everything, which was terribly exasperating, but I knew that I was very far from perfect myself.

At any rate, one of my friends from the list was a gal who had joined a year or so before, named Bobbi. Bobbi wrote me offlist, during this difficult period, and urged me to call her sometime, if I needed support. Well, I'm not much for telephoning folks, so at first I thanked her and told her I would but didn't. These evenings alone were proving very tough, though, so one night I called Bobbi, and we had a nice chat. This became a regular occurrence, but I didn't make it through without also ringing up my old "friend," Mr. Bottle, and his buddy, Mr.Pain Pill. It didn't help that, in the midst of this marital breakup, my Mom got a pulmonary embolism, had to go on life support, and ultimately passed away on January 1, 2009. I was also watching my net worth go up in smoke, following the financial crisis, so it was tough times on many fronts. I didn't make it through all this sober, but with Bobbi's help I didn't go off the deep end either and was able to sober up and be there for my beloved Mother, when she most needed me.

I can say, very honestly, that I had no romantic intent when Bobbi and I began talking, and I know she didn't either. But, gradually, things began to change.

Eventually, we began to fall in love, despite never having met in person. When my soon to become ex-wife finally moved out in late January of '09, Bobbi and I started talking about maybe meeting in person, at some point. Bobbi bravely flew down to L.A., from her home in Eugene, Oregon, on March 6th, 2009, a date we still celebrate as our "meetiversary." She is truly the love of my life, and when I think about my luck in somehow stumbling into such a relationship, I am almost tempted to believe in a deity. I say "almost," because if such a deity exists, why hasn't he/she/it favored everyone with such good fortune?

I wish I could say that was the end of my drinking and using, but alas, no. Bobbi and I were doing our best to spend time together, but it was sporadic at that point. Later that year, in August precisely, I got the idea to attempt to refill my old hydrocodone prescription, which I had last filled in late 2008 when I had relapsed in the midst of my various crises. Amazingly, it went through without a hitch, and I was off-and-running again, only with one difference; now, it was a secret.

Of course, Bobbi and I were doing the long-distance thing, but we still talked every night. One night, not too long after I had begun my secret relapse, we talked, and afterwards I took some of my pills and began drinking, and was still drinking the next day, when I got the bright idea to ride my bike to a Pro Beach Volleyball tournament. One aspect of my unhealthy relationship with opiates, is they make me feel kind of wired, rather than tired. So off I went, without sleep, down to the beach in my car, and then onto my bike, and rode some miles up the shore, into Hermosa Beach. Once I got there, the prospect of sitting in the sun and watching volleyball had a lot less appeal than entering a local pub and having some beer. So, on no sleep, I commenced to downing who knows how many more beers, and at a certain point decided I'd better head home.

They say riding a bike is one of those things you don't forget, but those who say that haven't tried doing it while on an all-nighter with beer and pills. I got to a point where the bike path runs next to a hedge full of sharp stickers, which served as my landing pad when I lost my balance. Some kind onlookers helped me get to my feet, and then recommended I get to an emergency room as soon as possible, as I was bleeding from numerous scratches all over my body, including a few nasty ones on my face. I called my brother's widow, who was kind enough to pick me up and drop me off at a local hospital, where I spent the rest of the afternoon and evening, mostly waiting to get seen. At a certain point, when I thought I'd sobered up enough to pass, I called Bobbi to inform her of what had happened, although of course I omitted the drinking and pill-popping. So, I eventually got stitched up, and went home via cab.

Well, that's it, I told myself--I'm going to sober up, and when I get about thirty days, then I'll tell Bobbi and my support group, one of the LifeRing email groups, what happened. Since I had already concealed the truth from Bobbi that night, I wanted to get a little time, and then tell her. And since she was on the Safe list, I couldn't tell them either. I thought that the sight of my scratched up face would remind me every day to stay on track. I found out that, without a support system, it was hopeless.

Thus commenced the most shameful period of this whole sordid tale, which involved me sobering up when we got together, and resuming the drinking, etc., as soon as we were apart, all the while not discussing it with her or anybody else. This went on for six months, and for me that entire six months is my bottom. Sometimes, I began drinking at the Eugene airport while waiting for my plane back to L.A, right after she dropped me off, which felt particularly dishonest.

I take small comfort in the fact that I stopped celebrating milestones around then, and my participation on the list was, for the most part, limited to occasionally cheering somebody else on. I avoided explicit claims to specific amount of sober time. Still, I knew I was lying by omission, hated myself for it, and lived in mortal fear of being found out by Bobbi, and dropped like a hot rock.

Finally, in February of 2010, I called my old AA friend Mark, and suggested we get together. We booked a dinner together on a Tuesday, and my last drink was Saturday, February 6, 2010. A little bit into our dinner, Mark looked at me and told me that he had a funny feeling, when he got my call, that there was something wrong. I told him what I'd been up to and told him that I was determined to get sober again, and that I was terribly afraid of losing Bobbi, and in the process hurting her terribly, if I didn't get sober. I pledged to be totally honest with him, and that was about it. I think I subconsciously picked Mark, because I knew he wasn't going to start bossing me around about meetings, steps, etc., and that he was a very non-judgmental guy. I had known him since about 1985, and he had been sober over 25 years himself.

In a few days, he came to my place and helped me round up all my pills, and we went together to a dumpster and threw them away. This may not be an approved way of dispensing with opiates, but at the time I just wanted them gone. I assume they ended up a landfill somewhere. I called my doctor's office and "poisoned the well," as I called it, by telling them I was abusing the opiates and not to prescribe them anymore. I did the same with the sleazy outfit that was prescribing the diet pills, which by then I was also taking. All this was possible, not because of any program, meetings, etc., but simply by becoming accountable to someone, and having made up my mind that I didn't want to continue to be the lying sneak I had become.

The following month, still sober, I went to Eugene for another of my get-togethers with Bobbi. I wasn't sure if she suspected me or not, but I think she knew something wasn't right with me. I told her, and to my everlasting gratitude, she ultimately forgave me, although I'm sure it was not an instantaneous thing.

The next dreaded thing was telling my on-line support group about lying by omission for six months. I am forever grateful that I was welcomed back, although someone did acknowledge that "that must have been a very tough email for you to send". It was.

If I have learned anything, it's to never think I'm out of the woods, and to never take sobriety for granted, which is why I've remained active on the list these last nine years. When someone reaches out for help, and I offer what help I can muster, I am engaging my sober self, and reminding myself of the misery that awaits me if I pick up a drink or drug.

For a couple of years Bobbi and I were still long distance, but I remained sober, and then she moved down here in early 2012, and we were married later that year. These have been the happiest nine years of my life, which isn't to say that I don't still have problems. For instance, I had to give up racquetball back in '09, due to a multitude of joint and back issues. I still exercise nearly every day (mostly walking and weights) and consider exercise a sobriety tool. I've had some pretty serious pain issues over the last five and a third years, but I have yet to take an opiate drug, and have found out that I can get through pretty major periods of discomfort without them. I have a structural back condition that is significant enough that I've had spinal fusion surgery recommended by two orthopedic surgeons, but I'm happy to say that various non-surgical things I've done have helped ease my symptoms.

A couple of years ago, I suddenly started having some bad pains in my neck and shoulder area, and I'm happy to say I've gotten through this, also, without opiate pain meds.

I am eternally grateful to LifeRing, and in fact I'm inclined to think I would not be here today, were it not for my rather accidental stumbling upon it, 19 years ago. Of course, I know that not everyone finds true love in sobriety, or for that matter in life, and certainly those who find love in sobriety don't always find it with another person who is on the same path; many struggle with mates who seek to actively undermine their commitment, as on some occasions my ex did to me. I do like to think that I will stay sober no matter what, including if I were to find myself alone again. I have reached an age where I can easily envision how further relapsing could lead me directly to the grave. Not to be morbid, but I think about how I want to go out, and one thing I know for sure is I don't want anybody having to find me, surrounded by empties and pill bottles, and forever shaking their heads saying, "what a damned shame."

We used to talk about "resolving ambivalence" on the email list, and a few years ago a long-time LifeRing list member, Alceon, used a phrase I like better, which has become a mantra of sorts---she referred to "the Power of a Made Up Mind." I have come to see this as a key component of recovery, and it dovetails rather well with empowering my sober self, The Sobriety Priority, as well as Rational Recovery's Addictive Voice Recognition Therapy, which I learned about through the lists. These combine to give me my basic recovery philosophy:

Make up your mind that you're going to stay sober, no matter what.

If a thought comes to use or drink, refer to step one.

That's it—two steps. I don't know about will power, but I've learned to exercise won't power, when stupid, primitive impulses tell me to drink or use. That way lurks a world of miseries, the worst of which is the loss of self-respect. This way is life, and it's my one and only Magical Mystery Tour. The magic, and the mystery, not to mention the love and sadness, are in this unaltered reality, and are not to be found in drug-induced altered states. I've already wasted too much of my life. No more.

Story 16

Finding My Power
by Mary S.

The story of recovery is a story of light, expansion, discovery, freedom, triumph, and a heaping dose of dumb luck. It is a story of the process of demolishing constructs that don't serve us; the willingness to let go and allow transformation to occur. It's often a story of pain, as we go through the slow process of allowing the fabric of our lives as we know them, to unravel. It's a story of shedding old skins and coming to the truth of who we are. Every story of recovery is also a story of redemption and resurrection, and for many of us, the meaning is purely secular.

Sobriety, to me, was an unattainable state of being. It was something that occurred in the experience of "other" people; people whose lives were starkly different from mine. It was either for life's winners, or for those who found Jesus in smoky church basements. The best I could expect was to live out my life as the pathetic drunken creature that was my father. Whenever a talk-show host interviewed a celebrity who recovered from addiction, I quickly changed the channel. I didn't want to hear sanctimonious accounts of what their lives were like then vs. the supremely enlightened beings they are now. I knew I needed to quit but was clueless as to how that could be accomplished.

To suggest that my recovery has been attributable to a single source, be it my own inner resources, LifeRing, friends, AA, Rational Recovery, would be inaccurate. Indeed, I've mined gemstones from many resources, but one fact is clear: without the people of LifeRing, I'd still be drinking today. Of that, I am certain. The story of my recovery is not a static event. Over time I see things I did not see the day I took my last drink, and so my perspective has widened and deepened.

In my late thirties, I drank very moderately, but just prior to my

40th birthday, a romantic disaster left me unable to cope. With dreadful force, all the abuse from childhood that had been neatly stored in the back of my consciousness, suddenly marched forward, demanding to be dealt with, ... and... I... drank. From that first drunk, I knew I was in the grip of something I could not control.

At the time I started drinking, liquor was life's sole comfort. I was well-employed, but desperately miserable at a job that had no connection to my heart. At 48, I moved to California, and changed careers. I was now doing human service work, and my life, at last, looked like the life of which I had always dreamed. My income was a fraction of what it had been, but I went to work each day with purpose and a happy heart. I had emerged from the prison of my past and was living in the light.

So, of course, I immediately quit drinking, right? Wrong! Although the reason I drank was now gone, once caught in the undercurrent of addiction, the way out would require an enormous commitment and the support of others. I had neither.   My circumstances at this point, were generally happy. I had the job of my dreams. I was living in beautiful California and wanting for nothing. My attitude toward alcohol shifted from it being the facilitator of much-needed oblivion to the facilitator of my new, improved life. An introvert by nature, I was becoming the social butterfly of my neighborhood. Guests were abundant in my house and backyard, and alcohol was always served. So, rather than drinking to drown my unhappiness, I was now sipping Chardonnay in the warm California sun, and moving to hard liquor in the late evening. But the cruel reality of addiction is that it eliminates the power of choice. I did not drink because I wanted to: I drank because I was compelled.

During the 14 years that I drank alcoholically, I was fully functioning, rarely drank before 6 p.m. and was never so much as late for work. Unhealthy thought habits however were lifelong companions. Even in favorable life circumstances, my self-talk involved daily affirmations of depression, anger, and fear.

My husband's alcoholism lent a sense of normalcy to my

drinking, and we supported each other in our descent into the depths of our illnesses. Slowly, alcohol structured my life as though I was living under Martial Law. It imposed a strict curfew, requiring that I be home by 6 p.m. to tend to my ever-growing addiction. I went to work by day and drank by night.

Soon, concern about my drinking was consuming me. I was afraid of the health consequences. I was afraid of discovery. I was afraid of what would happen if I found myself in a situation in which I couldn't drink, such as a hospitalization. I didn't answer the phone after a certain hour as I knew I'd slur my words. Although I was a closet drinker, addiction was forcing me out. There were times I drove home drunk from a restaurant; drove to the store, tipsy due to insufficient booze inventory; and the list kept growing. I was getting desperate and taking risks.

One long weekend, my husband and I spent a few days in Vegas. After a lovely evening out and a "normal" amount of drinking, I got up at 2 a.m. to go to the bathroom but didn't wake up. In my dream-state, I recall spending hours going through miles and miles of curtains in the hall trying to get to the other side. (I later concluded that the curtains were in our room; and the process lasted less than a minute.) Apparently, I staggered across the room, passed the bathroom, out the door, and awoke to find myself urinating on the carpet in the hall. The level of my humiliation and horror left me nearly hysterical. I wanted to seek help at that moment, but, fearing a knock on the door by Security, my husband silenced me. I lay in bed, trembling and wet, the rest of the night.

In the light of day, my husband found the incident amusing. He assured me that what happened was completely normal. Being away from home, I simply got confused. It could have happened to anyone. Yeah, perfectly normal! Any sensible person would have ended their drinking career with this event, but the next night, a chair was placed in front of the door, and nervously, I drank as usual.

Over the next 14 months many significant but less dramatic events occurred, and on January 13th, 2004, I was sitting up in bed with my brandy, as usual. When my husband came into the room, I was in a blackout. I squinted my eyes and contorted my face to see him through what seemed to be layers of gossamer. I have little recollection but was aware that I was arguing with him. Cutting sharply through the haze, came the sound of his voice, dripping with contempt, calling me a "drunk"! I immediately fell silent. He, of all people, was calling me a drunk… and he was absolutely correct.

My first thought on awakening was that I'd had a very bad dream. But when reality struck, I was horrified. When my husband awoke, he was obviously pleased at the opportunity to lord it over me. He spoke to me, sternly about my behavior the night before. I did not defend myself. Instead, I sat at the edge of the bed and listened till he was finished. I then apologized, told him he was absolutely right and that I would seek help that very day. He hurriedly protested that he didn't want me to do anything so drastic and expressed regret at even mentioning it.

My workday had its challenges, and I was trying to rise to the demands while nursing a hangover. By 2 p.m., I started telling myself the same story I had told every day: "I'll just slow down and drink reasonably." But after so many failed attempts at moderation, I knew I was only deceiving myself. I picked up the phone and made the most difficult call of my life.

The guy at AA who answered, was a crusty geezer who had his fill of weepy callers. I told him I wanted to quit but didn't know how. He impatiently barked, "Ah, ya just go to a meeting". I needed better help than that, and so I nervously persisted. I told him of my insurmountable obstacle: the fact that I was married to another alcoholic drinker.

Under such circumstances, I expected him to declare sobriety an impossible task. But, after ascertaining that I wasn't in physical danger, he bellowed, "Let him drink! You take care of yourself first!" His words hit me right between the eyes. This dear man was giving me permission to go home and not drink no matter what. So powerful were his words, he may as well have told me to pick up my bed and walk.

Later, with great difficulty I got through the night without drinking. My husband thought this would be a short-lived inconvenience for him and so he tolerated it... sort of. He continued to drink as usual, before dinner, at the dinner table, after dinner, and in bed. After a week or so of suffering through the smell of my drug of choice, I asked if we could agree to make the bedroom off limits to alcohol. He agreed but came to bed each night reeking of my favorite brandy. No one promised me this would be easy, and it wasn't.

During my first 100 days I went to a handful of 12 step meetings only to discover that for me, they were more harmful than helpful. Spiritual by nature, I had many higher and deeper powers greater than myself, but they simply had nothing to do with getting or staying sober. As a person whose childhood was marred by abuse, I found concepts such as powerlessness to be downright toxic. And so, with no support whatsoever, I held on by the tips of my nails until one day, in a desperate online search for alternatives, I happened upon LifeRing. I signed up for one of the email lists, and for the first time in my life, felt that I was home. These people presented me with a sane, logical, no-nonsense, no BS, no excuses brand of sobriety. At that point I thought that abstinence would be a temporary necessity. Three or four months ought to do it, and then I would return to normal drinking. Over and over, list members reiterated that quitting needed to be a permanent state of being, one day at a time. With their repeated emphasis on "Don't Drink No Matter What", and the fact that sobriety would need to be my top priority, I was able to better deal with life, and issues related to my drinking husband.

I forget what it was called at the time, but I accepted LifeRing's offer of a Sober e-pal. The gal with whom I was matched was a High School teacher with 19 months of sobriety. I told her I was struggling, and she replied, "So, in other words, you're drinking." I assured her I hadn't had a drink in (approximately) 100 days. She paused, confused. "So, what's the problem?" she asked. "Well, the people in AA told me I'm not doing this the right way." "Nonsense!" she replied. "If you're not drinking, then you're doing everything right." She suggested that whatever I had done for those first 90 days, to "do it again". She spoke to me the way a seasoned teacher would speak to a nervous pupil. She calmly told me that if I could make it to 90 days, I could do it permanently. And here's the magic: I believed her; and so, it came to be.

The tremendous power of the word cannot be over-emphasized. As this story reveals, my recovery was greatly assisted by the words of two people: the cranky, but highly effective guy from AA on Day One; and my LifeRing e-pal on Day One-hundred. The AA guy was a rough and tumble old-timer, while my e-pal was a highly trained educator who used her skills to quietly reassure me. Words needn't be polished nor even well considered, as long as they're authentic.

I didn't need a cheering squad. I didn't need to have my little accomplishment exaggerated. I simply needed to be told I was on the right path.

Working on the Recovery by Choice Workbook, I was asked what I would place ahead of my sobriety. It gave several examples and when asked about marriage, I hesitated. My marriage was sacred; nothing could come before it. And then I got it! If I wanted to stay sober, sobriety would need to become the first priority of my life. Until then, the Sobriety Priority was just a slogan, but now it had a meaning that was supremely helpful.

I stayed sober by absorbing every word that was written on the list. I logged on several times a day, hungry for the words that would become the bricks I would use to build my sober house; to live a life of freedom. During the first three years, my sole means of sobriety support was on-line. There are those who would say this is not possible, but the quality of the posting was such that it completely met my needs. At three years, I started a LifeRing meeting in my city; and my sobriety grew to new heights. People sometimes ask how I got and stayed sober with a husband who was drinking in my presence for so many years. As I clung to the heart of recovery, I became willing to let go of my attachment to my husband. Either I would have to put distance between us, or I would have to relax my commitment to sobriety. I chose to make sobriety, not my marriage, my top priority.

As to how I got sober, I don't eliminate the possibility that universal forces provided opportunities that I had the choice to accept or reject. In the beginning, fear was the engine that ran my recovery. It was a healthy respect for the power of my opponent. I white-knuckled it when necessary. A list member once referred to "bottom" as the point at which we become sufficiently horrified. I had reached that point and was willing to do whatever it was going to take to get well. Each sober day gave me a little more confidence that maybe I could do this seemingly impossible task. As I strung those days together, I knew I didn't want to go back.

The stages in my recovery journey have been:

- Abstinence
- Acceptance
- Emotional Sobriety
- Recovery
- Ongoing Transformation

Like most people in early recovery, I wanted to rush the process, but each stage took considerable time as it took root and blossomed. When I was focused on the necessity for abstinence, it was easy to lose sight of all the good that awaited me. Seeing recovery as deprivation can cause a person to lose heart. Conversely, if I get too caught up in Transformation, I tend to lose sight of the basics. The bottom line is that, on one level or another, I need to be connected to my Sober Peeps every day. For me, that means staying connected to the email list, and attending a weekly LifeRing meeting.

In recovery, life showed up, as it does. At seven months, I went through the upheaval of an interstate move; at seven-and-a-half months, my 19-year-old nephew was killed by a drunk driver. I experienced the situational depression of not finding a job in my new state; and my husband of 20 years, who never once gave me cause for doubt, ran off with a woman 21 years his junior. I questioned my ability to survive, but within a few short months, accepted the new reality, and forgave him. Using a Roger Teel quote, I put an "expiration date on my bitterness". I challenged all negative thoughts and feelings and made decisions to cast off anything that was not serving me. And I gave myself permission to emerge with a level of joy I had never before known.

People sometimes refer to me as a "high-bottom" alcoholic. While it's true that I have not experienced legal or employment problems as a result of my addiction, had my drinking continued much longer, this story could be quite different. Tweak the circumstances of my Vegas fiasco just a bit. Had there been anyone in the hall at the time I staggered out the door of my room, I could have been arrested. Tweak the circumstances of my final blackout involving my husband. Had there been a gun in the room, I could be sitting in prison for the rest of my life. Everyone's luck eventually runs out, so when it comes to the horrors of addiction that I have been spared, I know I stand a good chance of experiencing them in their fullness should I pick up another drink.

There's a saying in Women for Sobriety that rings true, "You don't need to ride the garbage truck all the way to the dump". Because LifeRing helped me to eliminate drinking as an option, I was never seriously tempted to drink at or over anything. But what really got me through life's challenges were the new thinking skills I learned from my fellow LSRians. I came to recognize irrational thinking, and to replace it with thought patterns that served me. I released depressive self-talk, and now, at 65, find that I'm happier than I've ever been in my life.

Why the need for secular recovery? Like anything else, recovery is a cognitive process. Secularity did not diminish my spirituality; in fact, it enhanced it. I find it more natural to relate to others without the bias of spiritual interpretation. I prefer being with a group of people in which there is no religious-based hierarchy, where I don't have to concern myself with being "right".

I thrive in a group culture that emphasizes personal responsibility rather than reliance on and surrender to an external entity. Not only don't I care about anyone's religion or politics; for the purpose of recovery, I don't even want to know. Just as students with religious backgrounds can thrive in a public-school environment, so I thrive in a recovery community that isn't concerned with my spiritual path. I have encountered very few LifeRingers in my City who identify as atheist or agnostic. Some have chosen LifeRing because they prefer our group structure with cross-talk; others prefer our focus on the present, rather than the repetition of old war stories. Spirituality in a group setting can quickly turn into something that feels like religion, and that is something I would prefer to avoid.

Secular Recovery is about free will. In it, I find egalitarianism, tolerance, acceptance, and the absence of fanaticism. In it, I find not only an opportunity for a better way of life, but a responsibility to exemplify it. In a milieu that is non-directive, where the only absolute is the need for abstinence, I am able to discard old stories of lack and limitation, and to joyfully live life as it was meant to be lived.

Story 17

My Journey Started on a Stretcher
by Katie Gallagher

Where do I begin to share the story about my journey of sobriety? It is not a point in time. It is more like a blurry continuum of all the stops and starts--of the promises made in the dark as my body and mind cried out for an end to the madness and of the years of lost opportunities that will never pass my way again. This is a story of the thousands of lies told which I "thought" protected my secret, and of the many embarrassments that played over and over in my mind as the haze of boozy fog lifted. It's a recurring drama of obsession over whether I would always have access to alcohol. Will they be serving it? Maybe I should get fortified before the party? Then they won't see me drink as much. I was always making sure there was enough booze in the house for when I got home.

I was living the life of a lying slave: fearing every morning, drinking every night. Trying to hold on to a semblance of normalcy. Every sunrise dreaded. Trying to pull myself together to make it to work. Hearing the rattling of all my empties as the sanitation truck collected them. Not even embarrassed. Retching till I hurt for hours. I called them Zine mornings. Visine, Listerine and Compazine. Every day, trying to put Humpty Dumpty back together again to face a day at work. Will they know? I will be late again. Will they smell me or the 100 Altoids I've consumed? Will they notice my bloodshot swollen eyes no Visine could hide, or the lethargy and confusion that stimulants couldn't alleviate? The thirst and the Gatorade bottle on my desk. The trembling hands and the severe change in my handwriting. Coming late and leaving early.

These were the mile markers in my journey toward sobriety. I could not know that a day might come when I would be able to control this horrible monster inside me. But did I really want to live my life without a drink?

Then one day it was no longer an option. I knew the day had come when I arrived at the city hospital. I knew when I saw the look on my family's faces as they gathered around my stretcher while I convulsed uncontrollably. I knew when I saw the tears streaming down my little brother's face as he stroked my hair. I was down-- sick, tired and at the end of my drunken journey.

The day comes that you had been praying for. You wake up and ask, when did I actually arrive? And how did I make it there alive? When will I be safe? Will I ever have fun again?? Will I ever be normal? Normal? I was never normal anyway.

Now I am different but wonderfully alive. And with mental clarity, I have much more time to live. Yes, there is boredom as I find ways to spend the extra hours of my day: hours I used to spend sick, sleeping or drunk. My first year, I was too busy surviving to be bored. I spent hours online at meetings or in chatting and in extra hours at work, salvaging all the damage I did. Visiting family to reconnect.

Now in my third year it is time for me to rebuild my life. Get healthy. Move more. Show gratitude and pay forward. Talk more to God. Go back to school because I want to.

Work on my 25-year-old marriage, most of which was a drunken memory. Maybe I'm really a newlywed?? There is so much to accomplish in what time there is left. My bucket list is full and now I can empty it. Skydiving may have to wait awhile.

Story 18

I Was Ten
by Steve Snyder

I may be lucky to be alive today. And, no, that's not hyperbole.

I may be lucky to be alive today and certainly to be alive, living freely and, as much as is reasonably possible, living as myself.

This is my story.

By the time I was 10 years old, my dad had regularly given me and my siblings sips from his pre-dinner or dinner time beer. I had also occasionally unscrewed an already-open quart bottle in the fridge and taken an extra sip. But one day, my oldest brother opened the door to an upper-level cabinet in the kitchen and showed me what was on the top shelf. It was where dad kept his liquor. He got out the bottles and with the help of enough water to take the edge off straight liquor for a 10-year-old's tongue and stomach, I started sampling. I tried the vodka first. To the best of my memory today, it smelled kind of astringent, like rubbing alcohol and tasted about the same. Then came the gin. Growing up in New Mexico, I'd tasted juniper berries before, and gin seemed to taste like vodka plus juniper berries. Then I saw the whiskey. Bourbon. With that dark-amber brown color. Real men drank whiskey. John Wayne drank whiskey — straight. So, I had my brother pour me some whiskey as straight as possible.

And for a 10-year-old kid with an empty stomach it hit like a lightning bolt or liquid fire. But even though it burned, it didn't taste like rubbing alcohol or juniper berries. Plus, for a skinny, scrawny, and short 10-year-old, drinking Jim Beam as straight as possible was manly. I eventually drank about four to five ounces of what was three-quarters whiskey and one-quarter water. I couldn't wait to tell some friends about it. And luckily, I ran into a couple of them less than a block away.

"I drank THIS MUCH whiskey," I said, spreading my fingers wide. And I then threw up at their feet. So much for macho impressions to my friends.

Anyway, "friends" in general often felt like acquaintances. That's because most of them bullied me. And that's because, I'm venturing to say as an adult, to most of them I seemed like the white wolf of yore — an easy mark and one deserving of abuse. And that's because . . . I had an "unhappy childhood."

Without going into details, I am a "survivor." An adult survivor of child sexual abuse of incest by family members. Both of what is called "overt" and what is called "covert" abuse. As it happens, that same brother of mine had already shown me other facts of life before showing me where dad's liquor was. There was also a fair amount of emotional abuse at home and some bits of physical abuse. And as the youngest boy of four (plus a younger sister), it seems that besides abuse aimed directly at me, other emotions related to a dysfunctional family came my way.

With adult insight, I realize that by the time I was 16 I felt depressed. My parents had divorced when I was 13. Two years later I had moved with my dad from that rugged town in New Mexico to a high-dollar St. Louis suburb that we couldn't have afforded to live in if we had not been in academic housing while he went to graduate school. My younger sister moved with us but moved back with my mom after a year. I had already become depressed and alienated; that made it worse. I had already attempted suicide once, around the time of my first drunk. My mom and one brother had seen me and stopped the attempt. After that, it wasn't discussed further. Who wouldn't feel alienated and depressed after that? And more so after the culture shock a few years later with the move from New Mexico to St Louis.

At the same time, as a preacher's kid, I was in general the "good little boy," especially in upholding my dad's public image while chipping around the edges. I was getting drunk about once a month when I could during my senior year of high school. Getting high on pot about as often.

As for college? I had scholarships and other offers but felt so beat down and was such a people pleaser that I applied only to my dad's religious college alma mater and one other place.

There was some consolation, however. The school was in Kansas which was still an age -18 state for beer. I could drink legally after the middle of my freshman year and I bought beer often before that, since in a small town, all college kids were assumed to be 18.

I eventually graduated with a "useless" liberal arts degree, having developed more drift in life and having suffered some other emotional speed bumps as well. Continuing the post-high school theme, I eventually went to my dad's alma mater graduate divinity school. But two-thirds of the way in, I realized that self-honesty compelled me to not only not be a minister but also to admit that I didn't accept much of what I'd been raised with. I still got my degree while trying to figure out what was next, with new rounds of depression and anxiety weighing in. I moved back with my dad for a while and the feeling of "disappointing him" in my career decision probably further fueled my depression. Moving from the conservative wing of Lutheranism to secularism along with becoming more liberal than either of my parents, was pretty high-octane gasoline for my emotional downturn.

I wound up with the most serious suicide attempt of my life after moving back in with my dad. My drinking probably started accelerating at that point and worsened during the following nine months. I was doing adjunct college teaching and working part-time at a convenience store as well.

One night while on third shift there, I was held up with a big, menacing 9mm automatic by someone from an apartment complex nearby whom I suspected used marijuana and maybe other drugs as well. Scared indeed.

Well, I wasn't shot. After he left, I did step one of store procedure — I locked the doors. Before step two — call the police

— I grabbed a beer out of the walk-in coolers and chugged. I then called the police and chugged another while smoking cigarettes to try to cover my breath until they arrived.

Well, after that I felt a bit shell-shocked and started drinking on the job. I also began to feel resentful about how my life had turned out up to this point. I felt a bit adrift too. Usually I would pay for the beer though occasionally I either didn't or forgot to. Well, eventually I missed cleaning up all my empties and the inventory didn't tally perfectly, and I was asked to show myself the door.

Nothing was holding my dad in Michigan and with tightening standards for adjunct teaching, nothing was holding me there either. So, I went with him down to Texas and got started on the career path I've been on ever since. I got hired as a newspaper reporter. The editor and publisher there was - to use a stereotype - a Type-A male and to use another stereotype, a Type-A male alcoholic like the ones that AA worries about the most.

I let his pressuring and his personality wear on me and started drinking over lunch time. Then I occasionally started having a shot before coming into work. I figured that I smoked enough to cover up some of the aroma and he smoked enough to not smell most of the rest.

Eventually, after one too many "last straws," I found a new job as editor of "my own" weekly newspaper. And in part because we did not have an on-site publisher and for other reasons, my drinking hit its final 18 months of deterioration. I was a 24/7 drinker at this time. My only "choice" in the morning was deciding whether to start the day with a beer or a shot of straight whiskey, if I thought my empty stomach could handle it. I had gone further down the road in other ways; I was pacing my drinking by my smoking; I was drinking and driving; I was sinking further into a moderate, chronic dysthymia. And that was not all.

At about this time, the news came out that baseball Hall of Famer Mickey Mantle needed a liver transplant, and when he got one, there was speculation about him "jumping the transplant line." Soon after this there were reports that too much Tylenol or generic acetaminophen in conjunction with alcohol could cause severe and permanent liver or kidney damage. Having had "fast" suicide attempts fail before and thinking I might be too cowardly to try an even more serious attempt, I figured this was my shot at slow suicide — wreck my liver, not go to the start of a transplant line and get put in a hospital to die on a morphine drip. Yes, that's how I felt. I didn't even care. I even used the word "alcoholic" about myself in internal conversations at times.

Then I was fired for being a bit too anti-authoritarian or whatever in the chain of command at my newspaper company. I surely could have been fired for drinking on the job had the publisher of the daily paper been paying attention.

And then things changed.

My office manager had been teasing-flirting with me, even knowing I had drawn strict boundaries about that and had told her so. (She has her own story elsewhere in the book of life.)

Me getting fired removed any boss-employee issues. So, I asked her out and we started dating. And I kept drinking.

One day, however, she said the right things in the right way at the right time and I listened. And I stopped drinking.

Two weeks later, on the way to a job interview back in Texas I stopped in Amarillo for gas. And a voice in my head said, "Open the phonebook when you go inside."

I did. Among AA groups was one called the "Hobbs Plaza Group." Coming from Hobbs, New Mexico, without being too superstitious about it, I took that as a sign of some sort. In hindsight, any AA group with a name to which I could make a correlation probably would have been a "sign." Call it whatever I will today, I called it a sign at that time. I phoned the group and found out it had a noon meeting. It was about 11:45 a.m. so off I went.

Perhaps typical of AA groups, nobody called on me until the end, even though I was crying off and on during the meeting. When

108

someone did call on me, I said my name and that I thought I was an alcoholic. A few people talked to me after the meeting, gave me one of AA's 24-hour chips and I went down the road to my interview. I got the job — in a town too small for an AA meeting. But I found AA elsewhere — and something else. With newfound sobriety, I found old memories too.

Until this time I had only vaguely remembered --in "intellectual content" -- bits and pieces of the sexual abuse.

About the time I quit drinking and left New Mexico for the Texas job, more memories — complete with the emotional connections — came back in waves. At times I would be driving and have to pull over to the shoulder. I would start crying so hard. Silent scream nightmares and a few flashbacks came up as well.

Fortunately, I also found other help. In the next town of any size where my company's local group of newspapers was headquartered, I found a counselor with some experience dealing with child abuse cases. She was primarily a child counselor; she had never before dealt with an adult survivor. But she had some relevant experience. And that, as much as AA, was important for my healing. Probably more so.

I wound up with a diagnosis of PTSD. This was in the late 1990s, before the Iraq War and 9/11. When I read about it, I first thought it was just a "paper" diagnosis for insurance billing. But today, more than 15 years later, I realize how real it is. The various forms of child abuse certainly cause PTSD. And my dramatic move away from the religion and politics of my family of origin were an added traumatic stressor. Certainly, as described above, even without everything else, being the victim of an armed robbery itself would be a traumatic stressor. Even as sobriety started to sink in for me, I was restless.

At the same time, I was fortunate, especially for small-town Texas, to find an AA group that was not too highly religious. It was also good that on many a Friday or Saturday night, some members of the group I went to stuck around not for 15 minutes after the last meeting, but an hour or two to play cards or dominoes. But I figured things might be better in the big city, and I was hoping to get there for other reasons.

Well, before I could land work that would make that possible, I got fired. The details aren't important other than the fact that I eventually landed a new job in metro Dallas. I learned something from all of this, and I continued to stay sober.

After the move, a few good things happened on my sober living and sober growth journey. Quite possibly the biggest started while job hunting in Dallas. I found a clinic called "The Family Place." In addition to offering counseling for battered spouses and children in such families, it had group counseling for adult "survivor" of child and other sexual abuse. For obvious reasons, it ran these group counseling sessions as gender-segregated. It had one opening in its one male survivors' group, and I was in. I received years of help there. I learned more about how the abuse had affected me. I learned that I wasn't alone. Several other members were also sober; even if they were doing the 12-step route, we still had similarities. I learned how deep personality issues can be and not only how much alcohol or drugs can bury them, but also how much the pain that leads to drug or alcohol addiction can bury them before that. I also learned that alcohol hadn't been my only unhealthy way of coping with the pains of my past.

Above all, I learned to start letting go of shame. My tears over the first couple of years of sobriety had helped me do that with myself. Now, group therapy helped me do more of that with myself and start doing that with others as well.

The other important thing I discovered was that AA wasn't necessarily more broad-minded in big cities. There was an AA group halfway between my apartment complex and my office. Perfect, right? Well, it was perfect except for the fact that there was an actual Bible sitting on the coffee table at the center of the meeting area and that many members of the group didn't see anything wrong with it. However, at the time I was job hunting, I had also been searching for a secular path to sobriety which I continued to do after I moved. At a Barnes and Noble, I came across one of the books by Jim

Christopher, founder of Secular Organizations for Sobriety. I then discovered that SOS had a meeting in Dallas. It was most of the way across the city, true, but there it was.

This being the year 2000, I also got online at home for the first time and discovered that there were online AA groups. However, I discovered many of them were no different than face-to-face AA groups, with some of them being just as fundamentalist, if not more so.

But within a year, I also discovered LifeRing online with both the LSRMail email group and the LifeRing online meeting room. I eventually became an online meeting convenor, something I have done off and on for more than a dozen years from that time through 2015. LifeRing differs from 12-step sobriety in that it makes no pronouncements couched as "suggestions" about how counseling, psychological medications or anything like that must take a back seat to the 12-step regimen. I am very glad for this, since I've had anxiety attacks at times including big ones after job losses, and other psychological issues surely related in part to PTSD. And as a convenor, I try to remember to couch my suggestions to meeting attendees as being purely my own opinions based on my personal experience.

I want to end with that thought and related final insights. Not only will I never be perfect, neither will I ever be completely "healed." I know that and I accept that, not only intellectually but also emotionally. At the same time, I find that I can eventually move on from occasional sadness and anger.

That said, I know I can move on more easily with the counseling help I have gotten in the past, plus the support of LifeRing members in general and especially the support of those with similar backgrounds to mine.

To other readers, I cannot encourage you enough to get all the help you need to stay sober and to live sober. I still have issues with clinical anxiety at times as well as low- grade depression. But, I'm sober, and all alcohol would do is bury that anxiety or depression. It wouldn't help the pain beneath it. It wouldn't make things go away. Nor would it provide inspiration or insight.

Because of this and because of all of my story, readers, I want to tell you it's OK to cry, as well as laugh through life-- for women and maybe especially for men. Just stay sober while you're doing it and hang on as needed. If you need to "hang on" with the help of others, we're here.

Story 19

etude-itude
by m.k.

It is with great humilitude I'm asked to chart my gratitude.
I spew forth the platitudes. Rectitudes of necessitude,
They all reflect amaritude.

I'm told to change my attitude.

Looking at the longitude, I start to sense the magnitude.
Why not approach this work with aptitude, fortitude, and certitude?
Just watch me shed my assuetude!

And with it time in hebetude, days and nights of similitude.
I will trade in solitude; a sense of quietude will do thank you.
It is with definitude I give up the mansuétude
And with that, too, my servitude.

Today my choice is valetude along with its vicissitudes.

Story 20

Flight to Sobriety
by Hilary

Eleven years ago in August I boarded a plane from Liverpool UK to Portugal, where I was teaching at an international school. I was going to be alone for two weeks. I was going to stop drinking!

Of course, this was not the first time I had tried to do this.

I had my first drink, aged 14, a Cinzano Bianco Vermouth, on the beach on holiday in Beira Mar, Mozambique. I felt so grown up! By the time I was at art college, aged 17, I was eating my evening meal in the pub with half pints of beer, and when I celebrated my 18th birthday there, the legal age to drink in England, I was considered one of the regulars. Fast forward 20-odd years, and I did manage a couple of years without drinking, but only in England. When I went abroad, I allowed myself a drink or two, and strangely, even though I could drink myself silly on the plane home, I could stop the next day without a problem. This didn't last.

In my fifties I knew I had a problem, and I tried to moderate my drinking. I hated the hangovers, and I made secret deals with myself. My partner, also a heavy drinker, had heart problems. We tried to stop drinking together, but it never lasted. He liked to enable my drinking. I don't really know why, maybe because then I didn't notice if he drank. Sometimes when I finished a bottle of wine or whisky I'd say, "Oh, I just need one more". And he always had a bottle hidden in the trunk of the car or somewhere else.

So, what was different 11 years ago, after 40-odd years of more or less non-stop drinking?

The first thing was that I realized I had to stop drinking for my own health and well-being, not pretend and just say I had stopped drinking because I was supporting my partner when he tried to stop for his health. I knew I was in denial, and I was embarrassed to tell people I couldn't drink socially.

In those first two weeks alone in Portugal, I discovered LifeRing Secular Recovery online and joined two of the US lists, and the UK one as well. I read everything I could, all the tips to help me through withdrawal. When I look back, maybe the one thing that helped me the most was the notion of the lizard brain and imagining that it was a separate part of my brain. So, when the cravings kicked in, I was able to confront them and say "No".

At that early stage I did not believe I could manage a prolonged period of abstinence. But I got through the two weeks, and when my partner arrived back I told him I had stopped, and I wanted to stick at it. He agreed to stop again too, which was a great support for me, but this time I had to be brave enough to tell people I had stopped drinking because I couldn't just have one drink. I think at first, after the cravings subsided, this was the thing I found hardest. None of my friends thought I would stop long term, as I'd stopped and started so many times before, and naturally many of our friends are drinkers too, and they liked us drinking with them. I needed to regain respect as a sober person, and for them to realize I could still be good company without alcohol.

The LSR mail lists gave me great support, each one in a different way, and after a while I felt able to contribute to support others, often feeling a bond of shared experiences. I used the LSR chat room as well, and also began to chat with people whom I now consider real friends on social media. I had the Recovery by Choice workbook shipped from California to Portugal. The excitement I felt the day that arrived! I found the workbook very helpful in looking at myself, my triggers, and how I could prevent a relapse. Also, how to redevelop myself as a sober person.

Of course, those first few months were hard. Every experience where a drink had played a part was difficult: trips abroad, cooking, a family wedding, but gradually it became easier. Before I knew it, the months added up to a year! I realized that in social situations the drinkers hardly noticed what I was drinking as long as their glasses were full. I became much more confident in saying I was a person who couldn't just have one or joking that I'd drunk enough for one lifetime. You'd have thought I might have twigged.

I really feel that offering support to others can help one's own recovery. These days I stay with my English LSR mail group, but I still chat online to the many friends I have made around the world through LifeRing and can probably discuss issues with them that I would feel uncomfortable discussing with local friends. I have never been to a f2f meeting in my life, which I think proves that recovery is possible via internet support alone.

At this time in my life, I can honestly say that I do not miss alcohol in any way.

Story 21

A Prisoner Friend
by Tim Reith

Note: Some of this material is taken from part of a chapter I wrote for Marty Nicolaus' How Was Your Week, Second Edition. Additional material is excerpted from an earlier contribution I made to the LifeRing Newsletter. I correspond with several prisoners on an ongoing basis, but one is very special; he became a dear friend. We call each other "brother." This is a story about him and me.

My friend was addicted to methamphetamine and alcohol. When he was 16 years old, he killed another young man in a gang fight. He was tried as an adult for his crime and was sentenced to 20 years to life in prison.

He attended several AA and NA programs in prison over the years, but not believing in a higher power, he eventually contacted our Service Center in September 2011. Being an ePal volunteer, I agreed to begin corresponding with him. Having no computer access, all his letters are handwritten. The turn-around time for our letters is long, since each is sent by regular postal service. My letters are inspected when the prison receives them. In spite of this, we have exchanged more than 40 letters each. He has no means of copying his letters before they are sent, so I send a copy of each back with my next letter so that he will have a record of what he wrote. I keep his originals in a safe place. If he ever wants them, I have them all. And of course, my letters to him are on my computer.

The first years of his imprisonment were spent in solitary confinement. With time he was moved to several other facilities, each with decreasing levels of security. Last year a new law was passed in his state that allowed special consideration to be given to persons less than18 years of age but who were tried as adults for serious crimes that resulted in long sentences. This law applied to him, and after a parole hearing and recommendation at his local facility, the governor signed his petition. He was released in November 2015 after 21 years of incarceration.

He shows remarkable intelligence and insight in his letters. I arranged for him to receive the Recovery by Choice workbook and he has worked through several of its Domains. This is part of what he wrote about the Third Domain:

"I think that this Domain serves to remind us that we have all chosen life at last. The checklist means what it is to live. No longer can any of us choose to deaden our lives and claim ignorance. I love knowing that there is no going back after being enlightened in such a truthful way. I have chosen a life of sobriety, chosen to live. It is such a great feeling."

Later in that same letter he wrote:

"We must celebrate our successes in order to give value to our failures."

It's important for him to feel as though he is helping me, as I am helping him. I continue to emphasize that our letters constitute "two-way streets" and indeed they do. I tell him stories about my personal struggles, and he often writes back with advice. This is very special for both of us. My correspondences with many ePals are rewarding, but the letters that he and I exchange are very special.

Although "Choice" is paramount, good or bad luck plays a critical role. He grew up in a broken home, and his gang membership gave him a sense of belonging. Because my family was stable, I stayed out of trouble and remained in school (for a very long time!). But we both share respective struggles that are not all that different. Now he and I are on parallel paths, and we celebrate our sobriety together. I am quite certain that his sobriety (and mine) will continue. I share my feelings with others, but his responses to those that I share with him provide different and unique perspectives.

He has been corresponding with a woman for quite some time, and they decided to marry in prison. He was allowed to invite ten "special guests" to the wedding, and I was very honored to be one of them. It was a two-day drive but how could I refuse? I was the only non-family member present. I met his mother, his two brothers and their wives, and his aunts. After many years of estrangement, it was wonderful to see them all there.

The wedding was quite moving. He and his wife each wrote vows and read them to one another at the ceremony. Of course, it was a secular affair. Another prisoner took photographs. All ten of us were present. The next day I visited him and his new bride, again in prison. It was just the three of us then, and we had time to talk for a few hours. After many hugs, I went on my way.

Story 22

The Long and Winding Road
by Robert Stump

Prologue

One day in the early eighties, I was at home in the garage drinking my daily allotment of alcohol when my youngest son Nick found me and asked me to look at his homework. As we were going through the assignments, he looked at me at one point and said, "Dad, why do you always smell so funny?" I had no answer for him.

What he said really bothered me and I'd like to say I started my recovery then. Alas, that did not happen. I did not stop. I would continue drinking for another 20 years. It would be a long and very private journey into the depths of hell and eventually, with the help of Kaiser and LifeRing, I would climb back out into the world of sobriety.

The Start of My Journey

I was born and raised in the San Francisco Bay Area, going to the local Catholic grade school and high school. Growing up in the Bay Area in the 50s and 60s was an eye-opening experience. All around me events were happening that would soon shape my world-view. In the late 60s, I became "of age" and started partaking of some of the local addictive offerings, really minor stuff at the time, but a foretelling of things to come. I graduated from high school and decided I was going to college. With my parent's blessings, I went off to Austin, Texas in 1971 to continue my higher education. Boy, did that turn out to be an "education."

Going Down the Road in The Party Bus

I drank a lot in college and engaged in some sporadic drug use. The days were long, and the nights were even longer. I found that alcohol was my go-to drug, especially in social settings. It made me feel good, special, more charming and more socially at ease. It erased

120

all the awkwardness I felt when interacting with others. It was fun.

Needless to say, my academic performance suffered greatly. After a couple years of college, I came back home to the Bay Area and started working in the family business. I got married, bought a house, and helped raise five wonderful children.

During this time, I continued to drink, but not to excess (at least in my mind). Social gatherings were an excuse to have a beer or two (sometimes many). My wife and I would go to all the family celebrations: weddings, baptisms, birthdays, even funerals. The men in the family, and some of the women, were big drinkers, so I fit right in.

I remember one time going to Reno on a party bus with my wife and the relatives. I was the life of the party. We played cards and had drinking contests on the way up and back. I remember wandering the casino floor getting lost and confused, finding myself, at one point, in the public toilets puking my guts out. It was a wild time, at least the parts I can remember. This type of activity went on for years.

The Path to Hell

In the late eighties, I slowly sank into the black hole of true addiction. It was bad. I drank more and more, cycling back and forth in my behavior; one day being the good guy in the family, the next day being the drunken SOB. My bizarre behavior eventually alienated my children and caused my wife considerable hardship. The word "divorce" came up many times.

Though I had never been arrested, thrown out of the house, or fired from my job like some other people I knew, it was during this time that I realized I was a full-blown alcoholic. It was all I could think about. I had to make sure I always had enough liquor on hand for the day. Hangovers were increasing, the bottles were being hidden, and occasional blackouts were being experienced. In the back of my mind, I knew I had a problem, but refused to admit it. I couldn't have sunk that low.

The End is Near

In the story the hero confronts the threat, kills a monster or two and lives happily ever after usually with a pretty maiden in tow. It's all quick, simple, and easy but reality is a lot messier. It took me from 1997 to 2006, another nine years, and three tries through the Kaiser CDRP before I was able to conquer my "monster."

The first time I went through the Kaiser program, I attended the 90-day evening class. I participated in all the prescribed activities including the mandatory attendance at two outside recovery meetings per week for the three months I was in the program. As AA was the only meeting format available at the time, I attended lots of AA meetings. However, even after considerable searching, I never found a meeting I felt comfortable with. In fact, certain meetings tested my resolution not to drink again. The AA message never resonated with my philosophical outlook on life. I graduated and went back to drinking after seven months of sobriety.

About four years later, I went back to Kaiser for a second time. It was more of the same. I didn't even last the whole 90 days of the program. I started drinking three days before graduation.

Another five years went by and I was consuming massive amounts of alcohol every day. I wasn't feeling so good now. I would wake up with a hangover every morning and pass out drunk every night. I was getting sick all the time and throwing up blood. I finally went to the doctor and was told that if I didn't stop drinking, I'd soon be dead. This came as quite a shock. I remember thinking that I didn't want to die this way. I decided that life was much more desirable than death by drink. I had to find a way to achieve long lasting sobriety.

The LifeRing Way

I went into the recovery program for the third time with a very personal reason to succeed (the prospect of death will do that). This time I knew what to expect and what to look out for. I finally realized I had to take personal responsibility for my recovery. I applied myself with renewed vigor and became fully involved in

122

understanding my addiction. The group interactions and the educational meetings that Kaiser provided helped me tremendously.

I looked to the internet and read many books about addiction and recovery, gaining valuable knowledge and insight. It was at this time that I discovered LifeRing on the web. During my research of this program, I found three things I liked about LifeRing: One: LifeRing is an abstinence-based program. Sobriety is the number one priority. Two: LifeRing is a secular based, non 12-steps recovery program. People of all faiths and none get together to talk recovery and because the meeting is secular, there is no need to call upon a higher power to achieve sobriety – you have the power within yourself to live a sober life. And three: Self-Help - everyone in the meeting is encouraged to help themselves by doing sober activities that promote a clean lifestyle. This is done by developing a Personal Recovery Program – whether that means going to 12-step meetings, learning a new language, strengthening your relationship with your family and sober friends or volunteering to help out at the local soup kitchen – your Personal Recovery Program will help you embrace the celebration of sobriety, encourage personal growth, and become the map that will guide you down the road of life.

Now this sounded like a group I could relate to. It also met Kaiser's mandatory requirement of two outside meetings a week and was available locally – a win-win situation for all. I went to my first LifeRing meeting and never looked back.

The LifeRing meeting was led by a person who had at least six months of recovery time. People sat in a circle, facing each other and talked about recovery – both the good times and the bad times. There was a good exchange of ideas and methods that could help people cope with drinking and using. People spoke about what worked for them. There was no, "You should do it this way because it worked for me." type of talk. I listened, I talked, and I began to develop my own Personal Recovery Program, sometimes incorporating the "best practices" of others.

I felt connected to these people and understood what they were going through because I was experiencing the same things. The concepts of the 3'S: Sobriety, Secularity and Self-Help, rang true to my ears, and LifeRing's message of Empowering Your Sober Self really made sense to me. For the first time in my life, I realized that I could and should take responsibility for my own thoughts and actions. Life had become worth living again. After graduating from the Kaiser program, I continued going to weekly LifeRing meetings. After four years of attending these meetings, I ended up becoming a LifeRing convenor.

Epilogue

With the help of LifeRing, the caring staff at Kaiser, and a wealth of recovery knowledge, I currently have almost 14 years of sobriety (as of 2019). My quality of life is good. I have a strong relationship with my wife and our five adult children. I have no cravings or desires to drink at this time. There are still trials and tribulations that need to be dealt with, but with a clear mind and sound body, I can see the road ahead and negotiate the potholes a whole lot easier now.

Story 23

Making Sense of It All Twelve Years On
by James Ringland

Twelve years after my last drink, in 2007 (age 54 at the time), the world of alcoholism and "active recovery" seems well past. My connection with LifeRing – once regular meetings, convening, and some links to LifeRing management – is down to following a few on-line groups, running into folks around town I met in recovery, and going to an occasional party. Working sobriety is neither hard nor the focus of my life. I am aware I am – and must be – a non-drinker in a world where sometimes drinking is the cultural norm. I have personal patterns and family support in place to help with that. In short, I live in a recovery world now, nicely in the "maintenance phase," that works. And better (or worse) yet, I think I've made some sense of it all.

So what happened and what worked for me? And what sense did I make of it? The two sections below explore these questions. The first gives the story: a blow-by-blow of events, without too much interpretation, concentrating on my transition into recovery and the first year. The second, closely tied to the first, offers up some observations on the connections, tools, and intellectual explorations that proved most important in working through the active part of my recovery, in making sense of what happened, in identifying where I need to be now. LifeRing played a starring role, but a whole lot of other people, organizations, and ideas also contributed.

Events

I came to alcoholism late. My drinking started to creep up in my 30s, driven mostly, I think, by external factors. In my 40s, it gradually took on a life of its own, with nudges from elderly parent problems pushing the process along. While I certainly believe alcoholism is self-reinforcing, those who suggest addiction is purely internal – a dance between the person and the drug – aren't describing my experience. External factors played in too. It was a threesome.

I was a pretty typical "functional alcoholic": much of the time I was able to maintain family, career, and personal hobbies without too much trouble. Until near the end, heavy drinking was mostly a weekend and holiday thing. Many weeknights I didn't drink at all. Sometimes I could rein the drinking in for months at a time. Other times, I'd tell myself at 4:45 p.m. that I wasn't going to drink that night and find two glasses of wine under my belt by 5:15 … with more on the way. I even did some camping and backpacking during those years, with more of the latter in 2006, my last year of drinking, than any time since the early '90s. I didn't drink in the backcountry. At all. Don't ask about the campgrounds.

All hell broke loose in March 2007, courtesy of some problems in the workplace: lots of perceived responsibility in what turned rather quickly into a painfully chaotic situation. I began to drink even more. I was aware and a bit concerned that I was more on edge and less charitable toward others than seemed appropriate, even given the messy circumstances. I didn't relate that to the heavy drinking, but I knew something wasn't right. In the last week of March, I took a culminating business trip that had some really unpleasant moments. I stayed sober while I was there. Getting drunk in public was an unbreakable taboo. But when I got home Thursday night, I made up for lost time. Friday too.

Saturday was a little better, so on Sunday, April 1, I went hiking in a local park. I've generally been able to escape my troubles out hiking. Even when I was drinking, the trail was safe space and safe time. I'd found – and still find – a sense that I'm part of a much larger natural world out there. I experience the peace that comes with that. But on that fateful day there was no peace. I broke down crying over lunch and couldn't quite stop on the four miles back to the car. I came home and did the natural thing for an alcoholic seeking comfort: I drank. Wine. Only about a quart. At dinner I ranted to my wife how this all wasn't acceptable, how the job was driving me down, and how I had to get out of the situation I was in. She asked two simple questions: "Does your employer have Employee

126

Assistance Counseling? Maybe you should talk to them." And "How much have you been drinking?" Just a little re-focusing, but now my drinking and getting drunk were part of this messy discomfort too. It was very simple and very direct. And it hit at the right time.

I called the Employee Assistance Program (EAP) counselor the next morning to talk about the job problems (still, in my mind, the primary issue); my drinking (the secondary issue); and the sense I was showing signs of depression (probably a result of the work situation and a cause of the drinking). She was out. I left a message. I began to make arrangements to leave the work assignment that was causing all the grief, knowing that doing so might well impact my future career path. There was no return call from the EAP that day, so, with a call for help out there, I decided I really shouldn't go back in until Thursday. I had chosen a bad week to have a crisis. So once again I decided I really shouldn't drink until we met. And I didn't. On Thursday morning, we finally got together. She asked a bunch of questions, some about work but more about drinking. One brought me up short: "Think about your worst week. How much time did you spend drinking and recovering from its effects?" It came to 35 hours. I had taken on a second job: drinking. Her questions were very simple and very direct. And they came at the right time. I think at that moment, I internalized that I had a real alcohol problem. The EAP counselor completed the job my wife had begun, knocking down the barriers.

The EAP counselor urged me to enroll in a recovery program managed by my health provider, Kaiser Permanente in Oakland, California. I was shaken enough after my morning with her that I went right ahead: I had my intake interview that afternoon. The Kaiser folks proposed I start with a program of daily one-hour after-work meetings lasting about three months. There were some "class" sessions, but most were discussion groups. Their intensive two-week all-day program was an option too, but since I had managed to stay sober for a few days and seemed motivated, they suggested starting with the less invasive approach and I pledged not to drink.

Thursday evening, my wife and I went out to dinner with some friends from out-of-town, a dinner planned long before any of this came to a head. I had ginger ale, while around me the beer and wine flowed. It felt a little strange. But I had pledged not to drink. And I didn't. How very different from the situation just four nights before!

I attended the Kaiser after-work sessions. I can't claim instant enlightenment, but my journal entry for the day after the first session shows that even then I found bits of my own situation and my own patterns in the stories I heard floating around the room. By the end of three months, I concluded the program really had been a fine fit. I had worked through a lot. I had enjoyed the experience (well, mostly).

The Kaiser program required I attend at least two outside support group meetings each week. I explored Alcoholics Anonymous (AA) and LifeRing. I was most drawn to a LifeRing Recovery by Choice workbook meeting led by the book's author, Martin Nicolaus. For the other – or others, some weeks I attended more than two – I bounced around between a mix of How Was Your Week (HWYW) LifeRing meetings and AA meetings. This whole exercise – still working, the Kaiser program, and outside meetings – led to a very packed life for those three months. Maybe that was part of the exercise: no idle time to drink.

In June, I "graduated" into Kaiser's once-a-week meeting program. I continued with Recovery by Choice. I continued to mix LifeRing HWYW meetings and AA for the next few months.

I may fall into the category that William White – in his wonderful history of recovery, Slaying the Dragon (1998) – calls a "Pedestal Professional". I'm in one of those "professions that have historically been held to very high standards of personal conduct", although not in one of the groups White calls out: "clergy, health-care professionals, lawyers, and pilots". Scientists and engineers can also work in positions that society holds to higher standards. As such, I deal with both an employer and a certifying agency. When the certifying agency learned I was an alcoholic, albeit one in "full early remission", they pulled my certification ... four and a half months after I stopped drinking. (I was required to tell them I had entered a recovery program and they did various interviews.) That put my employment in jeopardy, although, as events evolved, my employer remained very supportive and pushed back on the certifying agency.

I asked for and got quite a bit of time to talk through it all at a HWYW meeting the evening it happened. To a lesser extent, I did so at other HWYW meetings in the following days. It was that event, and the enormous amount of positive support – as well as the just plain listening to a cry of anguish – that landed me in LifeRing for good. The combination of HWYW meetings and Recovery by Choice became my mainstay. Likewise, the Employee Assistance Program counselor who had worked with me since April provided a great deal of help through this crisis. She had professional training, some varied experience, and a "non-fundamentalist" twelve-step orientation that made the discussions an interesting counterpoint to LifeRing. Kaiser too was supportive, but they were a decreasing part of my recovery by then.

I ended up hiring a lawyer and going through a hearing process. The hearing was in March 2008, not quite a year after I entered sobriety. The bureaucracy churned. The certification was restored in July.

"Active recovery" lasted another two years or so, but I'll tread lightly on the specific events. Sobriety was no longer much of an issue but rebuilding a life and working on personal balance and personal understandings were. It is here that LifeRing played its largest role. I was sufficiently invested in Recovery by Choice that I began convening my own workbook meeting in February 2008. In the process, I built and rebuilt a personal recovery plan and worked through its stages. HWYW meetings were the sounding board for dealing with life events and for just being part of the recovery community. Attendance was up and down in my workbook meeting: lively active discussions in 2008 and 2009 led to long stretches of low attendance in 2010. The meeting folded at the end of 2010.

In 2008-10 I also got involved LifeRing management. I'll not work through the ups and downs here. In the end I learned I was a little too thin-skinned for much of that and that I could be a little too eager to try to go along with what people wanted, even if it didn't fit. I bowed out, and not terribly gracefully either. But if those LifeRing management interactions were a wild ride, they did give me a picture of what I could and couldn't do emotionally in my new, sober world: valuable information that can only be obtained by doing.

The double departure in 2010 – from convening and from LifeRing management – arguably ended the active part of my recovery. By then, maintaining sobriety was no longer a day-to-day problem. I had reestablished a non-alcoholic adult identity and a life structure that didn't include alcohol.

Connections, Tools, and Ideas

The last section of my story should make it clear that lots of different players had lots of different roles in my recovery. My wife and the EAP counselor were instrumental in moving me into recovery when my own discomfort peaked. Kaiser and my early regular interactions with the EAP reinforced my move to sobriety. Without them, I think it's entirely possible I could have concluded after a month or two that all was rebalanced, and it was "safe" to drink again. The Kaiser program also began the process of letting me explore my alcoholic past and build attitudes to move forward: things like living in the moment or viewing events from an external as well as a personal perspective. Many of those lessons were about things I may have done once but which had fallen away as I got more wrapped into my addiction. LifeRing came later. It had nothing to do with launching my sobriety and little to do with its early establishment. Not too far along, though, Recovery by Choice picked up the task Kaiser began, and became the primary tool (along with my journaling) for exploring where I'd been and where I was going. LifeRing's HWYW meetings proved to be the perfect fit to carry me through the employment crisis and the ups and downs thereafter. One of LifeRing's great strengths is its simple structure and tiny core doctrine: just the 3 S's – Sobriety, Secularity and Self-Direction - which means it plays well with other recovery entities.

As I look back, I see that there was more twelve-step influence in those LifeRing-centric active recovery years than I acknowledged at the time.

I didn't much take to the AA process itself: meetings with no cross-talk and too much ritual, plus a collected literature with a moralistic tone. The serenity prayer always seemed to me to present too strong a dichotomy: much (most?) in this world falls somewhere between having control and needing to accept. (Do you control the behavior of your spouse, partner, or closest friend? Or do you talk things out and have influence, even though you don't have control?) And, for that matter, what's a prayer and talk of God doing in a mental health support group?

But, as I noted earlier, the EAP counselor brought to my recovery a non-fundamentalist twelve-step orientation that trod lightly on "The God Stuff" but definitely pulled in many of its ideas. I thought about what she said. I read the literature. I found some patronizing and condescending. "We Agnostics" in the Alcoholics Anonymous book is pretty awful – but other parts had ideas I could work with, provided I was allowed to step back some from the literal details. Calling for a fearless moral inventory (Step 4) seems mis-aimed but calling for a fearless personal inventory is not. I wrote a long personal history that blended with ideas in Recovery by Choice's History Domain and my own desire to explore how the past influenced the present.

Even the idea of a "higher power" can work for me, if, as in Doug Althauser's You Can Free Yourself from Alcohol and Drugs (1998), which Marty Nicolas references in Recovery by Choice, I'm allowed to re-interpret "higher power" as "greatest source of support," or maybe as "greatest source of motivation". My EAP once told me that my hiking was my higher power. I did not disagree. The wilds have always been a source of peace and perspective … even spirituality … but more the spirituality of Emerson, Thoreau, or Muir than of Saint Francis.

A couple of other tools played a big role too. I've mentioned my journal in passing. Journaling has been my single most active recovery tool over the years. I started the day after my Kaiser intake interview, on their recommendation. I'm still doing it. The frequency and subject matter has changed over the years: daily and focused on specific recovery issues early on; more like weekly and focused on a mix of external events, emotional issues, and recovery plans in the later years of active recovery; an irregular and all-over-of-the-map mix in the last six years. Hiking, gardening, and photography notes now sit beside those discussion of events and emotions!

The Recovery by Choice workbook was the other major tool. I found lots of eye-openers among its exercises. The core tool of the workbook is the Personal Recovery Plan. I was building plans even before I got very far into the workbook: coming out of my Kaiser three- month program, I had a short list of topic areas and things to work. Recovery by Choice gave that process more breadth, depth, and focus. Each Domain ends with a call to identify the most important issue(s) and what specifically to do to address them. The book encourages focus: even that gnarly Feeling Domain offered up only eight blank lines for issues and five for actions.

I went through several iterations of rolling up the Recovery by Choice chapter plans, plus materials from other sources, into a single plan. I never quite followed the "Recovery Plan for My Life" section of the workbook, but I did follow its spirit by looking for connections, prioritizing, and trying to be specific. The structure I landed on about 18 months into recovery in October 2008 turned out to be the one I kept. It had six general elements. For each, I wrote a description, listed the hottest few issues, and called out one or a few specific actions to pursue. My discipline got better with time. The total number of actions went down but their specificity went up. I introduced some priorities. This is not the place to rewrite one of those plans, but the six topic areas may be of interest:

Reinforce Recovery – Meetings, convene, and check-in online.

Manage the Body – Weight management and conditioning.

Find Pleasurable Intellectual Activities – Early on, work and learning about recovery filled this. Today, add photography, nature study (mostly botany), and music (listening, not playing).

Find Pleasurable Social Activities – Work, family, and friends have always been the basis, but given my introversion, this one's been an on-going challenge.

Find Purpose – LifeRing interactions provided a focus here early on. Just taking care of the events and people in life can provide purpose too.

Find Peace – Yin to the all the Yang above. I mentioned finding aesthetic and spiritual calm in the wilds. Civilized things – music and theatre – fit here. There is an internal aspect too: finding personal balance, aligning my actions with my values and inner needs, and, indeed, simply being open to myself and others about what those values and needs are.

The details associated with each item on this list changed from year to year, as did the relative weights. Amazingly, as I look back at those old plans – they are in my journals – I did, or at least made progress on, most of what I wrote. (I was perennially over-optimistic about weight loss though.) I still revisit those six. This list works as the outline of a plan for life, not just for recovery.

One other thread entered into these active recovery years: an exploration of the nature and science of the addiction I experienced. Researchers can see organic brain issues – dopamine responses, reduced frontal lobe activity, and the like – associated with drug use and addiction. All that seems to model craving, tolerance, and withdrawal pretty well … but the layers of thinking underlying addiction, less so. I went looking for more.

A key early "aha" in all this came at the 2008 Life Ring Expo, when a talk by Dr. B. J. Davis, director of the Strategies for Change Substance Abuse and Mental Health Treatment Agency in Sacramento connected addiction with classical conditioning, an artificially and strongly reinforced classical conditioning. The standard discussion of addiction implicitly treats it as a disease (or something metaphorically like a disease) that is apart from, not within, the processes of regular human thought. But here, Dr. Davis said just the opposite. The aha? To understand addiction, understand "normal" psychology and motivation.

I pursued those lines quite a way and found what gets called "dual process theory of cognition" to be very informative. The model suggests we have two separate systems of cognition: a fast "pattern matching" or "reflexive" brain that drives action by immediate unconscious responses, feelings, and emotions, and a slower "logical" or "reflective" brain that combines memories and invents solutions to new problems via conscious, rational thought. (The ultimate general-audience, if weighty, discussion of the dual process model is Nobel-prize winner Daniel Kahneman's book Thinking Fast and Slow (2011), but a great deal of summary material is available on-line too. Kahneman calls the two systems simply "System 1" and "System 2".) The pattern-matcher is absolute: when it makes a match, it feels it has found something fully "right". The logical system provides rational oversight, stepping in if the pattern-matcher seems too far out of line and pointing out the shades of gray. There is virtually no discussion of addiction in the basic theory, but it is not hard to see addiction as the establishment of feeling- and emotion-driven patterns strong enough to set up self-reinforcing feedback ... and the weakening of the rational oversight. (The brain imagers can actually see addictive drugs weakening the function of the part of the brain most associated with rational thinking.) Framed this way, addiction is less a disease than a rogue pattern "programmed" onto a brain that is otherwise functioning normally. The programming is done by strong, artificially enhanced, self-reinforcing experience.

That seemed to fit an awful lot of what I saw in myself and in others during recovery. In the events of that first week, when first my wife and then the EAP broke down the barriers and when I refrained from drinking while all was on hold, I see a strong disruption of the pattern-matcher. I observe elements of behavior therapy in the Kaiser program: essentially a retraining System 1. The Addict/Sober conflict in LifeRing literature shows one set of matched patterns (the addictive ones) being pushed aside by another (the sober ones), with the rational mode of cognition weighing in with the latter (in the best case). One critical feature of recovery is simply gaining sober time. Unused patterns in the brain weaken with time. Indeed, building and reinforcing new patterns – new relationships, new activities, new interests, new expectations – is key. It is not surprising that Recovery by Choice deals with people, activities, feelings, and culture.

And with that, I'd come full-circle. Framing addiction within the dual process model of cognition, even rather simplistically, provides enough of an umbrella over what I've seen and felt that I'm satisfied. Addiction fits nicely as an artificially strengthened, self-reinforcing element of the pattern-matching mind. It's not something alien to the processes of normal cognition, nor something fundamentally mysterious. Passage through addiction and recovery can be seen in terms of building, reinforcing, conflicting, and replacing patterns, plus weakening and strengthening the rational oversight. LifeRing's processes – focusing on the sober self and staying away from the addict self, using the pattern-building tools in Recovery by Choice, and finding mutual support in the How Was Your Week meetings – fit right in. twelve years on, it all makes sense.

So, where am I? I'm retired. I hike, I backpack, my photography hobby is getting expensive, and my wife and I have travelled some. Concert going is almost a weekly affair part of the year. I don't go to recovery meetings or fret much about temptation lurking around every corner. Many of the situational techniques I learned in recovery – separate feeling an emotion from responding to it, try to be non-judgmental, be "in the moment", don't obsess (or at least find ways to hold the obsessiveness to short periods) – are pretty much worked into my behavior. That little dark voice encouraging me to drink is not 100% silent but so far has been easily shushed. I don't think I look like a "person in recovery." But if you define recovery as building a full and rich life that doesn't happen to include alcohol – the best definition I know – I'm there.

Story 24

I Call Myself Sober
by Byron Kerr

Never mind how far down I went. We may all have those stories. I can tell you a story about a best friend who came home in a box due to an overdose. I can tell you a story about my felony drug conviction. I can tell you a story about jail. I can tell you a story about a failed marriage. If you and I ever meet at a café somewhere, I may share some of those stories. The story I am going to share with you today is about my decision and commitment to be clean and sober.

One of my first attempts at sobriety involved voluntarily asking for assistance from my employer/union Employee Assistance Program (EAP). I had no DUIs and no work performance issues, but I was attempting to save a flawed 35 year marriage. I had researched local rehabilitation offerings to find a program that offered a choice of secular support. When I suggested a program that offered LifeRing as a choice, the EAP counselor said, "No." I conceded to the rehab program prescribed by the counselor, but I was both frustrated and angered by the denial of choice. I drove myself 100 miles to the prescribed treatment facility, which was very cleverly named, "A_ _ _ _ A_ _ _ _." I spent the next four weeks in near agony because of the constant indoctrination and complete lack of respect for my world view. The fact that my wife delivered the final message to me that the marriage was over while at the facility made me feel completely betrayed. My brother, who also visited me at the treatment facility, also refused to respect my need for a different path of support. Needless to say the "spin dry" did not succeed.

After the failed treatment, I fell into a downward spiral of daily blackout drinking. I had little to look forward to. The desire to change was nearly nonexistent. The only area of focus that I had in my life was getting through my divorce with as little pain and harm as possible. Even though the focus on divorce kept me going, it was

136

not a positive focus.

My marriage of 35 years had collapsed, largely due to my drinking. I had moved out of my home and was living a very lonely existence working a dead-end job with little hope. My friendship with Ken was one of the few positive points in my life.

My story turns around an event that happened with, Ken. We had been best friends for decades. We met as neighbors in suburbia. We raised our kids in the same schools, went to local events together, and visited each other's homes regularly. There were dinners and parties with food, wine, and liquor. Our kids grew up and moved on with their lives. I moved out of the neighborhood where Ken lived, but we remained close friends.

Ken and I share an enjoyment of backpacking, hiking, and camping. Since approximately 2004, we had planned the same, very specific backpacking trip every year. The destination was an alpine wilderness area in the high Sierra, within Yosemite National Park outside of the Tuolumne Meadows trailhead. Every year when the chosen date arrived, something had forced us to change the plan. We had never successfully made this specific trip.

When the chosen date arrived, Ken and I left his house at about 4:00 AM with his car loaded with all of our backpacking gear. We were finally going to make the trip. Cathedral Lakes, here we come! At last.

We had traveled over an hour away from suburbia toward the trailhead destination when Ken pulled the car over. He looked at me directly and said with tears in his eyes, "Byron, did you bring booze?" When I answered, "Yes," he turned the car around and headed back. The trip home was almost entirely silent. The Cathedral Lakes trip didn't happen that year, either.

Ken had seen enough of my behavior over the years. After he dropped me off, I committed to myself to stop, to quit, to abstain, to redefine who I am.

At the time, I was almost a year into a new romantic relationship with Christine. She understood my aversion to the predominant sobriety support. She was an amazing addition to the support I received from the people close to me. We remain in a committed relationship to this day. We destroyed all of the alcohol that was in the house at that time. I have not consumed alcohol since that date. I will not consume alcohol or non-medically indicated drugs. I gave myself a new identity. I am sober.

I knew that I wanted to find support and I knew that I was not able to find value in the predominant support model for myself. I had become aware of LifeRing from previous flirts with sobriety. I immediately began attending some of the LifeRing face-to-face meetings near me and completely enjoyed the experience.

Another challenge I was facing at the same time was that I had made a plan to pursue an educational goal and begin a new career. The school that I had chosen was in an area where no alternate to the predominant support model was available. When I arrived in the town where I had chosen to go to school, I only had five months of sobriety. I inquired with the LifeRing service office about starting a LifeRing meeting and they encouraged me to go ahead and make plans for a meeting. I was told, "By the time you get all the necessary components assembled for the new meeting, you'll have the required six months of sober time."

The first LifeRing meeting I started began on March 26, 2012. There were only three people there, myself included. I am eternally grateful to the two others in attendance. Since then, I have started numerous additional LifeRing meetings in several areas. Most have become vibrant and thriving meetings and stand on their own. Sometimes no one shows up. A few meetings have failed. Oh, well. I persevere.

As time goes by, my drive for continuing as a LifeRing participant and convenor is about much more than just my personal sobriety. I appreciate and draw strength from the LifeRing meetings I attend and convene. There is another reason why I remain active, as well.

I succeeded in recovery after finding support that was in line with, and respectful of, my personal worldview. I remain active in LifeRing largely to help increase the availability of clear and equal choice in recovery support. I firmly believe that when an individual is allowed to choose their own support model, they will immediately become invested in their choice and their chance of success will increase.

You can call me any number of names, labels, or titles including alcoholic, addict, or substance abuser. Any of these are OK with me if you choose to use them. I choose to call myself sober.

Story 25

Chemistry 101: Re-balancing the Equation
by m.k.

It's the hardest work I've ever done, stopping.

For the longest time, I thought if I could figure out why I was drinking too much, too often, I could figure out how to stop drinking too much, too often. It really didn't occur to me that I wouldn't be able to figure out why I was drinking too much, too often until I stopped drinking — really stopped drinking — long enough to attain some kind of balance and perspective.

Finding that balance and perspective has been hard work, too, but nothing like the work of early, early recovery. What ended up being extraordinarily helpful to me in the first few weeks of recovery was learning enough about brain chemistry and addiction to realize there were chemical reactions that were going on in my brain and body that I could do nothing to change.

Nothing, that is — unless I stopped putting alcohol into my system.

Why was that an "aha" moment for me more than other things? I'm not sure, but I think it has a lot to do with confronting the confusing perplexities of addiction and recovery from an objective place — brain chemistry — that had nothing to do with guilt, shame, embarrassment, or the state of my spiritual life.

My understanding of brain chemistry is rudimentary, at best. But being able to frame being in the throes of active addiction, and then the everyday tussle of early recovery, in terms of taking a simple constructive action (not drinking) to stop a series of chemical reactions was huge.

Of course, there was — and continues to be — other work to do: mending relationships, rebuilding trust, reconnecting with myself, and reconnecting with the world. And that work seems to shift and change as I continue growing back into the person, I lost track of for many, many years.

Stopping drinking or using takes courage. Recovery takes perseverance, hard work, and patience. But for me, recovery did not take belief in anything or anyone than myself (and. I hasten to add, a rudimentary understanding of the laws of chemistry!).

Story 26

Lost (and Found) in Margaritaville
by Patricia Gauss

"You're going to make me go to bars?" I still remember my horrified reaction when a longtime friend suggested that I hang out with her and some of her friends in order to meet people. It was the '80s, I was a newly separated twenty- something, and clueless about how to be single.

I'd never been much of a drinker, my experience limited mostly to the syrupy sweet, coming-of-age concoctions like the Singapore Sling or Sloe Gin Fizz, and an occasional glass of wine. I also had grown up with an alcoholic father and had recently run for my life (literally) from an abusive alcoholic husband. Suffice it to say, ~~that~~ these two very significant life experiences left me understandably nervous about alcohol and the people who drank it.

I also remember my first real buzz, and the warm, happy sense of well-being that washed over me. The anxieties of a lifetime were swept away with a couple of wine spritzers. I wanted to feel that way forever, and remember thinking, "So this is what it's all about." Likewise, as am introvert by nature, I was delighted to find that suddenly I could meet, talk to, and make friends with people without being horribly awkward.

Though I was already well aware of how alcoholism runs in families, I told myself that it takes YEARS to become an alcoholic. But I suspected, even on the day of my first buzz, that that I was going to have a problem at some point in the future. How long would it take? Would I know when I reached that point? Would I have to quit? Would I turn out like my father or ex-husband? As I began my own journey down the road of alcohol addiction, a part of my brain was always trying to pinpoint when that would be. When would I have to give up that luscious feeling forever?

My life virtually revolved around drinking from the very start, from the guys I dated - often, drinking was the only thing we had in common - to the friends I kept. Even my relocation to Florida about 5 years after my "awakening" was fueled by Jimmy Buffett music and visions of cocktails at sunset on the beach. I did, in fact, move to a beach town, where I could walk to and drink at seaside bars. This was how I made friends when I got to Florida. The atmosphere of beach and hotel bars, and the clientele that went with them, was so much more respectable than the smoky, smelly atmosphere of a local watering hole. I felt like I   was "living the dream," and the whole beach scene made it much easier to normalize my drinking and ignore what was happening to me for several years.

Fast forward to early 2003. I had arrived in the place I'd been dreading for so long. I'd been drinking every day for at least 15 years, with an occasional "dry spell" of a couple of weeks (just to prove I could). But the defining moment, for me, was when it got physical. I frequently found myself driving to work feeling shaky from the previous night, wondering if I was still drunk or just hung over, having dizzy spells when walking, and the worst thing, an awful feeling of anxiety that made it hard to leave the house at all.

I quite literally wanted to drink all the time. I would start each day resolving not to drink that night, but by lunch time I was craving a drink so badly that I often considered going to a bar during my lunch hour (I never did), and counting the minutes until the end of the work day, when I could go home and pour myself a nice big glass of red wine on ice. This cycle repeated itself every day for several months and the anxiety became almost unbearable. Finally, I knew I just couldn't do it anymore. I either needed to quit, or I was going to have to give in entirely, meaning drinking in the morning, sneaking a couple of drinks at lunchtime, and basically maintaining a buzz all day long. My own conscience wouldn't allow me to do this.

Even so, somehow, I wasn't quite convinced that I was an alcoholic. I'd done a lot of searching for a definitive answer to what constitutes alcoholism; some of it fit, some of it didn't. The defining characteristic for some of those assessments was, oddly, whether one

143

had gotten into trouble because of drinking. I never had, though I'm sure that there were many occasions when I could have gotten a DUI.

One of the sources of my ambivalence (denial) about being an alcoholic was the fact that most of the people I hung out with drank a lot more than I did. I was not a "typical" alcoholic in the sense that I could never drink the enormous quantities of alcohol that many were capable of, and I didn't indulge in hard liquor all that often. I didn't drink to get stupid drunk; I drank for that happy buzz that I described earlier. In fact, I was the only one ~~that~~ who seemed to think I had a problem. Even one of my regular bartenders, whom I knew to be a sober alcoholic, couldn't believe it when I tried to articulate my problem to her by saying, "It's not about the sunsets anymore, it's about the drinking."

At any rate, I found enough wiggle room in the definition of alcoholism that I was reluctant to identify myself as an alcoholic. What I did know was that reaching the point where I entertained thoughts of drinking as soon as I woke up meant this game was over, for now anyway. So, I went to the Internet and started looking for a support group. I couldn't bear the idea of going to AA meetings; I didn't see how religion was related to recovery (I still don't). And I really wasn't too interested in going anywhere in person. I wanted an online support group, and I didn't want to involve God in the discussion. I found LifeRing Secular Recovery, which had a couple of Yahoo groups, and even a local face- to-face meeting in my area, so I joined that group. It was so much easier than the walk of shame into an AA meeting. Tom Shelley, the "Listmeister," introduced me to the online Yahoo group, and within a couple of hours I had several messages welcoming me.

My plan was to quit drinking the following Monday. I decided that would be easiest, at least for the first few days, because I always felt the crappiest after a weekend of drinking, which usually involved afternoons, followed by a nap, then evenings. I related this plan to the group, and though several members urged me to stop right then and there, a couple of them supported my plan. And so, I stuck to my plan and did quit, on Monday, May 5, 2003.

I was very involved with the group during those early months. Up until the time I quit drinking, I had no social life to speak of beyond my drinking-buddies, so quitting drinking also meant losing all my friends and finding myself home alone with a whole lot of time on my hands. In those early days of sobriety, I devoured "recovery lit," books like *Drinking, A Love Story* by Carolyn Knapp, *Sober…and Staying That Way*, by Susan Powter, *Dry*, by Augusten Burroughs, *Out of the Rough*, by Laura Baugh, *Keeping Secrets*, by Suzanne Somers…I still love reading recovery memoirs, as long as they're not too heavy on AA-ism.

Once most of the cravings and whining were behind me, there was ~~also~~ a lot of introspection and navel gazing, certainly not necessary to the process of recovery, but something that many do, maybe because we spent so many years obsessed with drinking. Or maybe it's just all the extra time I found with no way to escape from myself.

I began dating right away, too, sooner than I should have. Thanks to Match.com it was no longer necessary to go to bars to meet people, and what followed was a string of short-lived "relationships." Suddenly I was over forty, and the guy pool was overflowing with excess baggage, parents with exes, tweens and teens and complicated custody arrangements. Not something I was good at navigating.

I had put my non-drinking status in my Match.com profile, so the guys I dated were not big drinkers for the most part, but at some point, I hooked up with a guy who was a "weekend warrior" type. He was fine with my sobriety, as long as it didn't interfere with his drinking and weekend partying. I should have sensed trouble from the beginning, but He had never been married, had no kids, so that made the whole thing so much simpler, from my perspective at the time. He was a nurse, so he worked long shifts, and I was often alone in his house, where there was always a good deal of beer and wine in the fridge. I resisted for a long time, but ultimately, I decided to see if I could drink again. I had been sober nearly three years.

He belonged to a kayaking club, which seemed to be ~~more~~ mostly about partying after the paddling events. It was after one such outing, sitting at a bar, that I decided to have a couple of wine spritzers. I can't really blame him; my ambivalence finally got the best of me, and I wanted to see if my prolonged abstinence would enable me to drink normally. I knew, from others' experiences, that it wasn't likely, but it was something I needed to find out for myself.

The experiment, as I called it, lasted about two months. Though I started out reasonably enough and drank mostly wine spritzers in a valiant attempt to keep the quantity of alcohol down, within a few weeks I was appalled at how many wine bottles (the big ones) were in the recycling bin at the end of the week. I was also starting to experience the anxiety again, which was probably the worst part. This time there was no denying it. I had to quit, again, and this time for good. So I set my day again, April 24, 2006, another Monday, just a couple of weeks before what would have been my third sober anniversary.

What followed was what has been called a "pink cloud," a period of a few weeks during which I felt great, my ambivalence gone, the question answered, and finally the motivation to LIVE a sober life, as opposed to just being sober. I no longer needed the support group as much because my internal struggle was done.

In the years since that fateful experiment, I've never been overly tempted to drink. It's no longer an option, not now or at any point in the future. It's off the table, so to speak, and I really don't think about it that often anymore. I've had my share of difficulties since then, layoffs, the loss of my house, bankruptcy (during the recession years of 2008-2010), and a more recent bout of severe anxiety that lasted two years. Still, I haven't craved alcohol as an escape route. If anything, the anxiety reminded me of how bad it got at the end of my drinking "career." I also met my husband, but at a local dog park, not Match.com. I had just weeks earlier cancelled my account and decided to scrap online dating for good. Part of that plan was to pay more attention to my dogs and start taking them to the park. Within a month, I had met the man who would become my husband. Just like they say, it happens when you least expect it…

In the end, it doesn't matter what caused my problem, whether it was genetically predestined, or simply the result of putting alcohol in my body every day for almost two decades. I don't know when I "crossed the line" into alcoholism, clinically speaking. It could have been the physical dependence, or it might have been years before. Clearly, I was mentally hooked from the very first buzz. Non-alcoholics generally have a take-it-or-leave-it attitude, might even leave a drink unfinished in a restaurant (an alcoholic would never do such a thing). I still feel like my "experiment" was necessary to resolve my ambivalence and make a commitment to lifetime sobriety. My only regret is having to subtract 3 years from my continued time sober. Also, I never go to the beach anymore, which is kind of sad, because it was the one place where I was truly happy. But I have such strong associations with drinking and the beach that I no longer feel comfortable going there. Maybe someday that will change.

I'm grateful that I found LSR, and though I'm not very active in those online discussions anymore, I am still in contact with many of its members, whom I consider good friends (and I don't throw the word "friend" around lightly). Even though I've never met most of them in person, I hope to change that at some point in the near future by attending an annual meeting.

Story 27

Sober in Sapporo
by CA Edington

How could I be an alcoholic? Alcoholics end up jobless, homeless, or even in jail. Yeah, I drank - a lot! But I was advancing my career as an educator and even getting two masters degrees, all under the influence of alcohol pretty much every day.

As a PK (Preacher's Kid), I grew up with no booze around me. People on both sides of my family were teetotalers. Not having a TV or seeing people drinking in my everyday life, I thought not drinking was the norm.

When I was five years old, I was invited to a picnic by my best friend in kindergarten, Carolyn. While we played, balancing on rocks to cross a small stream, the mothers set out the picnic lunch on tables in a grove, then called everyone to eat. To my astonishment and horror, the fathers were drinking beer! It was the first time I recall seeing anyone actually drinking any alcoholic beverage. After we ate, Carolyn and I decided to see how far we could go downstream, and her father started to follow us with a beer can in his hand. I was really scared because he was acting kind of funny, as though he was trying to play like a kid. To my relief, he couldn't keep up with us.

By the time I was 10, we had moved to a different town in upstate New York.

That summer vacation, I went to a friend's house and watched as, from her pantry, she brought out a can of beer and opened it with a churchkey. With the curiosity of 10-year-old girls, we took a sip. My mouth puckered at the vile taste. I couldn't imagine how anyone could even drink the stuff, much less enjoy it. Mischievously, she took a few more sips, probably more to get a kick out of my reaction than for the taste or effect of the beer itself.

Those were my only experiences with alcohol until I was 20.

I did a complete turnaround about my third year of college, also my first year of rebellion, including leaving the church. I can never forget my first drink, a sloe gin fizz, offered by a professor at a party at his house. It was scandalous not only because I was underaged, 20, but also because this was a small Christian college where drinking - or even dancing - was not allowed. After the party, I got back to my dorm room all warm, fuzzy, and giddy. I sat next to my roommate, babbling and in a garrulous mood, which threw her for a loop since that hadn't been my nature before.

That was followed by many more off-campus parties at which I drank, feeling less inhibited each time. Initially, not understanding my own limitations, I often drank to excess (I pity the poor guy who had to hold a basin next to the bed where I lay while barfing), but gradually I learned to pace myself, although I'd always drink all evening. To my delight, I became part of the sophisticated, academic crowd, the one that would sit around discussing literature, listening to jazz, or dancing. At that time, there was plenty of smoking as well, but my focus was on drinking, as well as which boy I was going to end up with. One act of rebellion involved my boldly walking through the campus with a friend, who was the president of the student body, smoking cigarettes; other friends were aghast at our behavior, but there were no repercussions since hardly anyone else took notice.

Fast forward to the first year after graduation, when, to my mother's horror, I got a job at a bar & grill where I'd serve booze. (There weren't many job openings for someone with a BA in English.) It was there that I first learned about cocktails, since I had to serve them to customers, and on dates I'd be ordering Black Russians and daiquiris while everyone around me was drinking beer. I ended up being a pretty expensive date! However, wine was my beverage of choice throughout most of my drinking career. In one particularly embarrassing situation, I was sitting at home drinking cheap wine when I got the idea of calling in on a talk radio program. I was so drunk that they had to cut me off and started playing music while the D.J. suggested privately to me that I get a good night's sleep.

That was followed by graduate school in Denver a year later, at which time I continued drinking pretty much every night. Whenever I moved to a new place, the first thing I'd do is scope out the nearest liquor store - actually, "stores" - plural, because like so many alcoholics, I'd rotate the places where I'd buy booze. I don't think I really fooled the liquor store clerks, partly because I would buy wine in gallon jugs, always making sure I had enough on hand. I'd even get those cheap boxes of wine - something I'd never let my snooty connoisseur friends know about - since, after the first three or four drinks, it all tasted alike! One bottle of wine was never enough.

I drank a lot of beer as well, not because I liked it all that much but because it was cheap. I was majoring in theater, and after rehearsals and performances, I'd join others at the local bar where we'd drink Coors by the pitcher until closing time at 2 a.m. At this time, I never thought of myself as a problem drinker, even when my roommate took me to the emergency ward one weekend because I was having a breakdown, supposedly over a paper I was writing. My delusion may have been because, despite my drinking, I aced most of my classes and succeeded in getting my graduate degree. How could an alcoholic manage that?

Throughout my marriage, and, a few years later, teaching, I continued drinking on a regular basis, always making sure I had enough in the fridge to keep me going until bedtime and even panicking when I didn't have access to alcohol. I recall a time when a snowstorm in upstate New York was so bad it covered all the cars in the parking lot and blocked the door to our dormitory. I still managed the following day to wade through three-foot snowdrifts to the nearest liquor store to stock up.

I was extremely focused on alcohol, more than my marriage or friendships, but never gave it a thought that my drinking was abnormal. I'd sometimes try to cut down, for example, filling my wine bottle with one-third 7 Up before going to a BYOB party, but I'd always end up drinking much more once I got home. During those years I also tried smoking weed, but it sometimes made me paranoid and left me feeling much more out of control than alcohol did, so I'd only smoke it occasionally.

There was one particularly harrowing time when I took an overdose of some OTC sleeping tablets. I was so frightened that I called a hotline but was told it was not serious enough to necessitate a trip to the emergency ward and just to sleep it off. The next day my vision was so blurred that I couldn't see the school number in the phone book in order to call in sick, but I finally managed. One concerned older teacher advised me to see a psychologist. I did so, reluctantly, and he noted the marks on my wrists where I had cut myself with a razor numbers of times but never enough to do much harm. Although he advised me to get further counseling, I never did, still not realizing or acknowledging that my problems were serious or that I was an alcoholic.

Often my drinking led to other uninhibited actions, one of the less innocuous being stripping down to my underwear and jumping into a community pool during a wild party at an apartment complex. I would also drive home from parties at other people's houses late at night, sometimes so drunk that I'd be seeing double. This was before most people were familiar with the terms DWI and DUI. On top of that, my drinking led to a lot of poor decisions when it came to sex with men, eventually leading to a divorce. It was merely by chance that I never ended up being hurt - except for a mild case of herpes - or in an accident.

When I moved to Japan to teach there, it was like heaven for an alcoholic. Drinking was - still is - the norm for most social occasions. In fact, when I would go out for drinks with my students after class, I was considered the guest of honor. Everyone wanted to pour drinks for the teacher, so I was constantly emptying my glass and holding it out for more, with someone always waiting to fill it. After all, that's what was expected! I didn't have to hold back, as I often had done at American parties, and would end up drinking twice as much as anyone there, but still seemingly sober and in control, much to the awe of Japanese friends.

A few years later, back in the Boston area and remarried, I started becoming more aware of having a problem. My then husband (a Thai man who had been my boyfriend in Japan) was appalled that, after drinking for a couple of hours, I would rush out to the liquor store to stock up before it closed at 9 o'clock. But even as I began to realize my problem, I continued to pride myself on being a controlled drinker. I never drank before or at work or, especially, in the morning, except for holidays like Fourth of July. Nevertheless, I did panic at the thought of running out of booze, particularly since the blue laws prohibited the sale of liquor on Sundays.

The time came when I knew I had to quit. I was again divorced and, by that time, had become literally a closet drinker. I had a housemate and would hide in my room in the evening to drink, leaving my empty bottles in my closet to sneak to the dump when she was gone. A couple of times I let myself run out of booze because I kept fooling myself into thinking that, if I didn't have any on hand, I'd quit drinking. On those occasions, I would sneak into the kitchen after my housemate was in bed and take down the bottle of hard stuff I knew she kept on a top shelf for guests. I'd have to check the label so I could buy the same kind at a liquor store to siphon it back into the bottle. I never knew if she figured out what I was doing.

I needed help, and I did try going to a nearby church that had AA meetings, but the smoke billowing out of the door kept me from getting even close to going in. For this and other reasons, I knew that AA simply wasn't for me. I wasn't someone who took well to following rules or even guidelines. After all, I was a person who had taught in a non-traditional school by choice, and I knew I needed some sort of alternative support in stopping drinking as well.

One day, in a newsletter that was distributed in our Unitarian Universalist church, I saw an ad for an organization that was an alternative to AA. By then I was so desperate that I wrote a letter all the way to California asking about any similar kind of support in the Boston area. I was extremely fortunate that a dynamic, enthusiastic young man by the name of Liam had just started up not one but two such support groups, and he was delighted when I contacted him.

I'll never forget the freedom I felt, with tears streaming down my face as I drove toward that first support group meeting in

Cambridge, Massachusetts. It wasn't the end of my drinking because, a couple weeks later I headed off to Japan for a six-week intensive teaching program, during which I drank (only in the evenings) just as heavily as ever - not very surreptitiously - buying the largest cans of beer available in the vending machine right outside my room at the program center.

However, when I returned to Boston, I was determined to start my journey in sobriety and set not only the start date, but also the time of 12:34:56 on 7/8/90. I was in my car at that moment and Tchaikovsky's 1812 Overture happened to be playing on the radio. I was practically screaming for joy as I celebrated the moment, because I knew that it was one the biggest decisions of my life and that it would stick.

I returned to the support group, SOS, an informed group of people who don't simply accept dogma without questioning it. There I discovered for the first time how secretive others had been about their drinking. I also learned that lawyers, police officers, counselors, teachers, journalists, artists, people in the military, and those in all walks of life were also alcoholics. I especially enjoyed our chats at Au Bon Pain in Harvard Square after the meetings and found myself looking forward to Sunday evenings.

Within a very short time, several other meetings had started up in the area, one for nearly every day of the week. I even contacted my ex-sister-in-law, who was a minister at the most prominent Unitarian Universalist church in Boston and arranged to have a meeting held there (which also meant that my secret was out to my former family). In a very short time, I had become a moderator as well as leading the monthly business meetings. I was totally committed to the group and to sobriety.

As soon as I determined that I was going to become sober, with some trepidation, I paid a visit to a counselor I knew on the campus of the university where I was teaching. I was assured that she would keep anything I said completely confidential. (Looking back, it's sad that my biggest concern at the time was that no one else know about my drinking. I had an excuse for not drinking at parties with colleagues because I always had to drive home.) She put me in contact with a female counselor at one of the major hospitals in Boston. In retrospect, I realize that (a) it was valuable for me to be seeing someone once a week because it reinforced my commitment to sobriety; but (b) the exercises she was giving me, probably from textbooks or lectures she had heard, were not effective; and (c) talk therapy was not for me. By mutual agreement, I stopped going after a year.

About that time, I had the opportunity for a life-changing experience through a five-day program called the Inner Quest Intensive and, later, other workshops including rebirthing and breathwork. Those took place at Kripalu Center for Yoga and Health, which I consider my spiritual home. However, at support groups I hardly even mentioned the spiritual growth I had gained by getting in touch with the true essence of my being through working through my fears in such intensive encounters. I would have loved to share those experiences, but I was aware that others did not share my beliefs and that what we had in common was alcoholism as well as drug abuse.

My story might have ended there, leading a sober life in Boston, but a couple of years later I got invited back to my old job in Japan. I remained sober, but it was extremely challenging with no support group and drinking being such an essential part of socializing in Japan. On one trip back to the U.S., I grabbed a glass of the free wine available on international flights when it was being passed around the cabin. Back in the U.S. I somehow wanted to prove that I was able to drink without adverse consequences. I have vivid memories of accepting a glass of wine at a small dinner party given by friends. I nursed that glass throughout the whole dinner, but a nagging voice within me kept reminding me that I was not a social drinker, and I couldn't bring myself to enjoy so-called normal drinking one bit.

Unfortunately, that was followed by five years of heavy drinking in Japan. The glass of wine on the airplane and the one at my friend's led to many, many, many more. I wanted desperately to stop, but I never succeeded in doing so for more than a day or two at a time. All the while, since most of my drinking was done at home after work, I successfully hid it from others and later discovered that my colleagues had no idea I was an alcoholic. However, I'd be so embarrassed by the amount of wine I was buying at my regular liquor store on the way home, when they kidded me about how much I liked wine, I'd mention "my friend". I don't think they were fooled one bit.

I tried going to an AA meeting in Sapporo, but language was a barrier, plus I came home reeking of cigarette smoke. Not my thing. There was also an English- speaking NA meeting run by someone I knew, so I decided to go. Three of us met at a Dunkin' Donuts. We had been chatting for at least 10 minutes, at which point the "real" meeting began. "Hi, I'm so-and-so, and I'm ..." Whoa! We'd just been spending time talking together. Why the sudden need to introduce ourselves? At that point the meeting became very formal, discussing some topic that I couldn't really relate to. I went back a couple more times but always ended up feeling like drinking more after the meeting!

I had a love/hate relationship with alcohol because I really did enjoy drinking, especially with a boyfriend who was also an alcoholic, although he would never have (and still hasn't) acknowledged it. But I desperately wanted out!

One day I received an unexpected email from Liam, the organizer of the support groups in Boston. I had lost track of him, but he sought to make contact with me. More importantly, he told me of an online support group. It was my only hope. I joined immediately.

I don't remember much about my first correspondence with the group, but I knew I had found my kind of people. Initially, I was still struggling with drinking but very open and honest about that struggle. One exchange, entitled "drinking at", got me to stop forever. It can be found in the archives called "Keepers" on the LifeRing website, but I'll quote it here:

Drinking "At"

By CA, Marianne H., Laura L., Marty N., Carol H.

CA began it on Sunday, 08 February 1998 15:36:

… I couldn't sleep because I thought I was going to have to suspend a student and ended up drinking. …

Marianne replied:

… Hope that next time someone gets in a jam, you won't punish yourself because of it…

CA responded:

I never thought of it as punishing myself, but maybe that's what I was doing. You've helped me see this in a new way.

Laura joined in:

I had a counselor who referred to this "phenomenon" as "Drinking AT somebody." During the time(s) when I was lapsing like that, it became very important to me to understand the connection between anger, sadness, and shame in my own life. Among others, I drank "at" a staff member who was ultimately terminated. I had given her every chance, encouragement, training, threat, cajoling, etc. I was angry that she was "doing this TO ME," I was sad because I knew eventually, she'd be let go, and I was ashamed because I felt that the failure was mine. I drank at other people too, but she really sticks in my mind for some reason, probably because of the fallacious argument within my own mind, and the faulty logic I used to make myself feel even worse. Hope this makes some kind of sense.

Marty chimed in:

Thank you for that expression, Laura. It really fits. I used to do it all the time....

Carol picked it up:

… Yesterday, I got angry with a friend and the first thing I thought of was having a beer. And then I remembered that someone on the list had said "I had a counselor who referred to this "phenomenon" as "Drinking AT somebody." That helped me and for once I didn't partake of my old friend. Thanks again.

And CA closed the circle:

Tonight, I'm trying "Being Sober AT My Students". In other

words, I want to be refreshed and clear for them tomorrow.

I felt very much at home with the group of people I interacted with on the list. Many of them have become close friends, even though we've never met face-to- face. When I heard of a LifeRing Congress being held in Florida in 1999, I jumped at the chance to go. Fortunately, I had the funds to travel at the time, plus it was held in February when Japanese university classes were not in session. I can't express how surreal it was attaching faces to the names I had seen in so many correspondences back and forth. I have to laugh because the woman I pictured as being short with dark hair was actually tall with blonde hair, and another I thought of as being tall and slender with long, straight hair was actually rather short and stocky with curly hair.

The bonding that took place at that event, which was very much like a retreat, was unlike any I've felt. Although we came from many walks of life, we had the common experience of what it takes to get sober, and we understood one another in a way that those not having experienced addictions simply can't understand. We also didn't have to spend time that weekend getting to know one another because we had already done so through the email list, and there was an immediate feeling of intimacy. On top of that, since this was the Constitutional Congress, along with other attendees, I had the privilege of signing the document that brought LifeRing Secular Recovery officially into being.

I also attended three other congresses, in Berkeley, California, and again in Florida until the date was changed so the annual meetings started taking place in the middle of the first semester of the school year in Japan, making it impossible for me to go. That didn't stop me, however, from meeting other LSRians whenever I could.

Less than a year after the first congress, I traveled to France to spend time with members of the email support groups living there, mainly ex-pat Americans whom I felt close to. Many people, especially Japanese friends, find it difficult to believe that I flew across the world to stay with people I had never met in person, both near Paris and in southwest France. However, I felt a strong connection immediately, to the point that we've become lifelong friends, and I've gone back to France to visit a couple of times.

As I continued my journey of sobriety back in Sapporo, I gradually told a few close friends about my no longer drinking (it being especially easy with one friend who was Baha'i and didn't drink because of her faith). My big coming out was at a meeting of international women who had bonded for other reasons, specifically facing what it is like making one's life in a foreign country where one is always considered an outsider. That kind of life especially takes strength in Hokkaido, where non-Japanese can feel much more isolated than in areas such as Tokyo, which has large numbers of people of many nationalities. The women in this group all have what I would consider a pioneering spirit.

That particular meeting was held because of the premature death of the husband of one of the women, and it was held so she could share her experiences with the group. Before that, however, we went around the room for a check-in. I glanced at my good friend with a questioning look. Shall I? Then I proceeded to tell the group that I was going to start a support group for alcoholics in Sapporo. I'm happy to say that no one was startled by that announcement, even though they had been unaware of my history of alcoholism, and several have since told me how much they admired my courage.

I prepared for the first meeting of the support group, setting up signs and making announcements, not knowing if anyone would attend. Fortunately, I was able to use my own classroom, but I envisioned sitting there alone. Just a couple hours before the first meeting, I got a hesitant call from someone interested in coming. I assured him about the anonymity and also that it was a secular group where we wouldn't be discussing religion. It turned out that he was the only one who attended with any frequency, but a couple others came now and then, and I was in contact with them via email or phone, sometimes even running into them in person. (Sapporo is a small city, even for one with a population of nearly 2 million.)

Eventually I couldn't continue the group because of too many commitments, and two of those who had come have now returned to their home countries. I felt some satisfaction in providing a way for a few people to be able to find others to communicate with in English, knowing they were not alone in facing their addictions. I still wish I could do more.

Meanwhile, I have continued to deal with going to parties and events where drinking is not only the norm but somewhat expected for those not driving. (Excellent public transportation in Sapporo makes it very easy to "go drinking".) One was actually a champagne dinner and I discovered that I was the honored guest, expected to make the toast! I did so with water, not allowing myself to be concerned with what others might have thought. On another occasion, the reception for a calligraphy exhibit, when it came time for the toast, everyone was holding a glass of wine, but I refused to, even though a couple of the hostesses kept trying to thrust one in my hand, saying it was just for the toast. They finally poured me a glass of oolong tea, and everyone breathed a sigh of relief that we could continue with the toast. Although I felt some discomfort, I didn't have the slightest qualm about committing such a huge faux pas in Japan.

I know that I've been left out of events, not invited because I don't drink, and I'm fairly sure I've missed out on some job opportunities since I don't frequent the bars where the non-Japanese, mainly males, hang out. However, my not drinking has been accepted more and more, and now people will often go out of their way to make sure there is some non-alcoholic beverage on hand.

In my university classes, I have talked freely about my not drinking, especially when the topic of addictions comes up in one of the textbooks I use. One would think that students might be rather startled by my history of alcoholism, but instead they end up focusing on their own addictions, everything from shopping to Internet use. Naturally, I talk about support groups and how much it helps having a mutual friend or friends in whom one can confide and even with whom one can make a pact not to engage in certain behavior.

For me sobriety is now a way of life. I have a huge number of sober friends from my support group, many of whom I've never met face-to-face but feel as though I know better than friends from my own city. Although I continue to read the Yahoo! group email messages on nearly a daily basis, I interact with many friends in other ways, primarily through Facebook, and our discussions are about what's happening in our everyday lives. Most of those friends have been sober for at least 5 years, and alcoholism is no longer an issue, even though choosing to be sober is what initially created a bond among us.

What I would like to see is the day when alcoholism is no longer a stigma, including that alcoholics are not imprisoned unless they are involved in a crime beyond that of drinking. I also hope that research will unfold more about the causes of alcoholism, resulting in treatment that is adequate and appropriate.

Meanwhile, let both those for whom some lubrication helps in relaxing, whether alone or in social situations, and let those of us, for whom such lubrication acts like a poison, find more "high quality" ways of improving our lives.

Story 28

Three SMART Stories

Introduction

We are three men in New York with different backgrounds, different problems, different strengths and different ideas about what is good for us. What we share is a desire to change and to adapt to whatever life throws at us.

We meet regularly because each of us has decided to pursue sustainable change and to support others who have made a similar decision for themselves. We seek helpful, lasting and evolving change through attending SMART (Self-Management and Recovery Training) Recovery® meetings in person or online and using SMART tools as we live life.[1]

The bedrock of SMART is stated in the program's tag: "Discover the Power of Choice.™" This is the point: You choose, within reason, what is most helpful for you in your abstinence-based recovery.

The phrase "within reason" is a second fundamental driver of our approach to recovery. The tools and techniques practiced in SMART meetings are evidence-based and can help to build and maintain motivation, deal with urges and manage strong emotions without reverting to addictive behavior. The aforementioned techniques are largely derived from CBT (cognitive behavioral therapy) and REBT (Rational Emotive Behavioral Therapy) which is considered a form of CBT. The key qualifier for any tool that is included in the SMART Recovery is "evidence-based." As new evidence is verified, there will be updated or new techniques becoming available.

---

[1] We write of our own experiences in our own words and do not speak or write as representatives of SMART Recovery®.

Many people are drawn to SMART because it is "evidence-based" and regards belief as a personal choice. Others are searching for results—as anybody with a pressing problem can appreciate.

For me (I am the W of these stories), this statement from the program's handbook reflects the hopeful tone of my ongoing, self-directed evolution, which requires abstinence from alcohol:

We focus on the present – and what you want for your future – rather than the past.[2]

SMART Meetings

SMART meetings are called "self-help, peer-support groups." There are both face-to-face and online meetings (usually 90 minutes) that start with the reading of a short introduction of SMART, setting out the meeting structure and some essential concepts. The meeting facilitator[3] guides the group through the structure by keeping the discussion on addictive behaviors, making sure that everyone has a chance to participate and maintaining a rational perspective. A "golden rule" is that members show respect for each other.

Folks are asked to "check in," to describe the past week's "top-of-mind" challenges and/or successes. They are also asked whether they have specific events or challenges in the upcoming week that might affect their recovery and how they plan to manage this perceived challenge. It's common for people to describe lapses and what actions they might take to address these lapses.

SMART doesn't reset the counter to zero if a person lapses into addictive behavior. The focus is on getting back on track if a lapse

---

[2] *SMART Recovery® Handbook*, 3rd Edition © 2013, Alcohol & Drug Abuse Self-Help Network, Inc., dba SMART Recovery®, ed. Rosemary Hardin, p.1.

[3] A facilitator completes an approximately 30-hour, 8-week "Distance Training Program" online and has to pass a final exam. This training includes two online voice meetings."

occurs and to learn from it. Also, people are neither encouraged nor discouraged from announcing days, weeks, months, or years— whatever framing is most helpful to changing and improving their lives.

Following the check in is the agenda-setting part of the meeting: participants decide what elements in the check-ins were of particular relevance for further discussion. People are encouraged to exchange viewpoints with the aim of being honest about their own thoughts, feelings and actions, showing respect for others' feelings and behavior, and — perhaps most important and most difficult — by not giving direct advice to another person in the group. The intention is to create a "safe" atmosphere. For instance, participants can choose to use any name or no name. People are not required to name a substance or behavior that brought them unless they feel better describing their situation in more detail.

In my experience, the best facilitators are able to give the meeting to the members of the group, who then choose a SMART tool that seems to address any "themes" that may have come up during the check-in. If no consensus is apparent, the facilitator may pick a tool to work on. To me, using a Chalk/White-board and putting pen to paper is a valuable activity to develop ideas together.

The workshop portion of the meeting features discussion, brainstorming and personal thoughts about a SMART tool that helps in making progress toward one of the following program aims:

- Building and Maintaining Motivation
- Coping with Urges
- Managing Thoughts, Feelings and Behaviors
- Living a Balanced Life

After the workshop period is completed, the hat is passed while the closing statement is read. I always listen for "be patient and persistent." I identify with that.

Three Stories, Three SMART Tools

G's Story

G is the owner of a textile and surface print studio in New York City. He has worked in the city at a well-known marketing and communications firm. He worked in the Hispanic and LatAm Markets, creating marketing-communication strategies and materials for Citibank, Allied Domecq, Nokia, Mercedes-Benz, Bellsouth and other "name" companies. He is also a volunteer facilitator for SMART Recovery NYC and a SMART Recovery NYC board member since March 2014. He currently chairs the Volunteer committee. His final bio comment: "Pilot at heart."

Tipping Point:

To: Papá <XXXXXXXX@gmail.com>

No me dejen solo [Don't leave me alone]. *Estoy solo. tan solo.* [I'm so lonely.] *Nadie me da cariño.* [No one gives me affection.] *Pero Los quiero tanto.* [But I love you so much.] *Quiero que sepan que no les dejo de hablar por que no los quiero. Sino porque necesitaba pensar y desintoxicarme.* [I want you to know that it's not because I don't love you that I don't call. But because I needed to think and detox.]

Por favor dejenme saber si los puedo Skype mañana por la tarde. [Please let me know if we can skype tomorrow afternoon.]

Bendicion. [Bless me.]

So why this desperate email, something I'd never done before?

It starts that night, like many others for the past three years.

6 PM: Call my dealer and leave a "coded" message that I need to see him that night. I am planning to party hard with a group of buds and need the usual, four eight-balls: $1,400.

I will convince myself I am presentable enough to shuffle to the ATM. The endless four hours passes, and my dealer shows up.

My interior design is reminiscent of pre-Giuliani Times Square: gritty, dark and desperate is how my place looks. The motif I call Porn Square, dimly lit, set up to put visitors at ease, most light coming from a sensory overload of porn coming from three screens: a 40" Flat screen, an old 45" projection screen and a 100" projection on the last open wall.

Futons on the floor in order to increase sexual real estate and drug paraphernalia throughout for easy access. To round up a group, I obsessively scour multiple gay hookup sites and text past tricks from my phone. I take more hits and answer messages both on and offline.

The prep for that night is halted by the remix version of Bruno Mars' "Just the Way You Are." Out of nowhere, I start crying and as the song progresses I am reminded that NO ONE, especially not me, loves me the way I am. I am alone, so very alone.

I desperately reach out via text to someone I know in Virginia who has been 20 years sober. She is my closest friend's sister's partner. I barely know this person. No answer.

So that's why the email.

To Decide

The following two months seemed like a movie. I was (but didn't know it) the protagonist. Hallucinations send me to the emergency room. I heard myself ask for help against the parasites that had invaded my body—a fairly common, very powerful delusion with Meth. People scratch their skin off. Diagnosis: "itchy arms". ITCHY ARMS!

A knock on the door. It was my cousin's partner, a shrink. I opened the door, then was convinced to go to the emergency room again. I assume the shrink's status would result in me being treated differently than on my earlier emergency room experience. But as I walked into the Bellevue's psych emergency room, a cop stood at the entrance.

I spent the next 17 days in the psych ward at Bellevue, 20 West. I was given bipolar medication. I didn't know what was or who was who. Twice a day I was asked if I was suicidal. Twenty five patients were held in a rec room which had a TV, a radio, a telephone, and a ping pong table. It made me wonder how they expected crazy people to not lose it completely when it was impossible to have a moment to think, to make sense of things. After a week, I wondered if I had been in the ward all my life and the memories of my life were inventions of my mind to escape.

My parents came from Guatemala to visit. I refused to see my cousin who, to me, was a jailer. Most importantly, I wanted out of the hospital. I was given an option: Go to an inpatient rehab of their choosing or stay at the hospital. I chose rehab.

Strip, squat and cough. That was my welcome at midnight at AFR (a rehab) in Michigan. The difference here was that people gave me the first sign of my having some choice. I was asked but one thing: to be open minded and try everything at my disposal. This became the cornerstone of my life in rehab.

Walking

Fast forward four years.

A curious thing happened to me walking back from the gym this morning. Besides feeling good from the endorphin kick, I noticed deliberate, controlled steps. A comfortable stride that allowed me to move forward at my own speed. My humble purpose was to get back home.

In Manhattan at 8:30 AM, you encounter a wall of people, most not looking up but at their mobile devices. Folks are dashing, darting, swishing, scuffing and cursing rapidly between slivers of space just to get to their destination a second sooner. Despite the fact that I am pumped, the gentle breeze from passersby brings a smile to my face. That morning, the pace was mine

According to Livestrong.com at 6'4" my stride is 26.56". Most of the time I am able to comfortably keep up with friends that are 6' or taller. Their stride is 29.88". To me, this was a symbol of my game of catch-up when with others. I tested measurement more recently. I walked a block next to a man standing at 6'4". By the time he turned the corner I was halfway down the block

But that day coming home from the gym, I felt joy and satisfaction unimaginable four years before. I realized I had rewired myself to slow down. No need to keep up. After all who in the sea of people would I be catching up to and, more important, why?

This has been one of the most valuable lessons learned in SMART Recovery, using its many tools and concepts: Despite the fact that others are passing me, I don't despair. It's my path, my chosen pace. In SMART Recovery I learned this skill by practicing Unconditional Self-Acceptance. I do not rate or label myself based on one action, one triumph or one mistake. All the walks I take comprise the whole that makes me "me."

Keeping My Cool: An ABC

My unhealthy behavior is four years behind me but the nervous excitement of what my life may throw at me lies ahead. Through the practice of the SMART Recovery tools, patience with my progress and (mostly) unwavering perseverance, I've worked towards those qualities I've chosen, qualities that I believe make me.

Something I use every day—it has become a habit—is a tool called an ABC.

The aim of an ABC is to recognize unhelpful, irrational, thinking that leads up to taking a drink, becoming angry, or reacting to any experience in a way you later decide was self-destructive or not helpful. Maybe you even feel regret. I have lots. The chain-reaction goes like this: Activating event>Belief generated>Consequent feeling/action.

Below is a Rational Behavioral Therapy worksheet I used to do an ABC. Writing it down by hand or typing is a very effective for me in "rewiring" or "imprinting" the brain. Structuring the concepts in language, by writing down these concepts, and in a way that makes sense to you—this activity itself can help you change. You can do your own research on the function of the parietal lobe and language, or you can keep practicing the tool until it's first, rather than second, nature!

As you might see, even when I work my way through the exercise the goal is not to eliminate the unhealthy negative emotion but to lessen its intensity into a healthy negative emotion. Discomfort—that's part of life—but I've disputed my underlying,

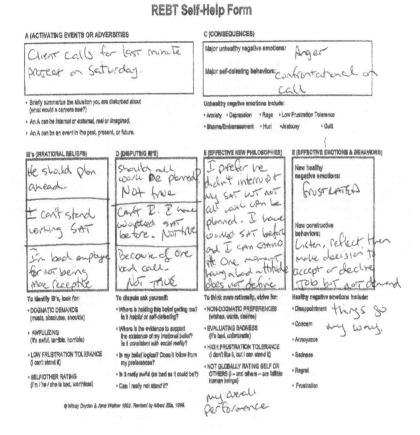

irrational belief about a specific experience. Basically, I decided it wasn't realistic to think that the rest of the world should/will do what I want. By the way: still at 5'4" yet emotionally feel 6'4"—not that there's anything wrong with my height...lol.

P's Story:

I grew up with a mother who was addicted to alcohol in a household that teetered on the verge of bankruptcy more than once. Teetering is uncomfortable at any age.

I turned to food, especially junk food (sweets, salty snacks such as potato chips), to comfort myself and to stuff down, literally, my growing anxiety and depression. In a nutshell, I started to binge-eat and overeat compulsively.

Inevitably, I became overweight and then obese, and established a habit (read: addiction) of overeating and binge-eating that stayed with me for the following decades. Despite these challenges, I did finish high school, left home and went to college, and ultimately attended and finished graduate school. In the process I moved from Germany to the United States.

I worked for about ten years in academia, and then switched to work in the pharmaceutical industry. While I knew that this line of work would entail several compromises, I hoped it would reduce the near-constant anxiety about job-security I had experienced in academia. However, my struggle with anxiety continued, as did my obsessive-compulsive overeating and binge-eating.

Intellectually, I knew my eating had taken a significant toll on my physical health. But the constant pressure to "increase productivity" had merely replaced the pressure to obtain research funding. I now understand that I had developed an anxiety disorder. A change in position and a change in employer in 2011 did not remedy this situation, and actually made it worse. Finally, a serious medical crisis brought things to a head and forced me to stop working. However, while this was a scary and even traumatic experience, it also motivated me to take that much-quoted look in the mirror.

I started psychotherapy to deal with my emotional upsets and my addictive behavior (compulsive overeating and binge-eating). About two and a half years ago, I also decided to attend SMART Recovery meetings, which offer help for people with any kind of addiction and addictive behavior. SMART recovery teaches and uses evidence-based CBT-derived tools and techniques to support recovery from any type of addiction and can be both an alternative and/or an add-on to psychotherapy, prescribed medications and 12-Step programs such as AA, NA or OA (overeaters anonymous).

I found SMART so helpful that I became a trained SMART meeting facilitator. I have led between three to five meetings every month for the last 15 months. The combination of therapy, attending SMART meetings, and using the SMART tools proved to be very helpful. I am happy to report that I am now "normal weight" for my height, and my cardiovascular health has much improved. I continue to be amazed how similar our struggles are despite the many different forms how our addictive behavior manifests.

Personally, I also enjoy SMART meetings because they are attended by people from all socioeconomic strata and racial backgrounds. Both genders are represented, attendees' ages range from the twenties to the sixties and even seventies, and meetings are attended by people from all sexual orientations. I greatly enjoy this variety, which, in my view, reflects the universal challenge of addiction and addictive (obsessive-compulsive) behaviors, regardless of gender, race or socioeconomic status.

Basically, it's good to know that I am certainly not the only person who is working to maintain motivation and resist urges.

Oh, and about the aforementioned SMART tools: Some of my favorites include the cost-benefit-analysis (see example below) -- also widely used in the business world—the urge log (exactly what is says, I keep a log of my urges to binge or overeat to learn when, where and with whom I am when I get the urge to overeat), and the Change-Plan worksheet. You can see those and several others in action at any SMART meeting. Some people don't like the word "tool" - I do. All of them are tried-and-true ("evidence-based") techniques to address the key challenges to our recovery. And, just like a physical tool - a screwdriver or a hammer - they only work if we put them to use.

Well, so far so good. I still find myself not practicing "my" SMART tools as much and as often as I would like, but also know that perfectionism is a common trait amongst people with addictive behaviors such as myself. Basically, I try my best not to give myself permission to slack off, but I also don't beat myself up for not being perfect (who is?).

After you read this and G.'s W.'s stories, please give SMART a shot (http://www.smartrecovery.org for meetings near you). You don't have to say anything in a meeting (always free to attend), and you can walk out if you really don't like it. Basically, the worst outcome is that you spent some time in a meeting that didn't resonate with you, but that still beats 90 minutes of gulping down junk food or alcohol, or smoking crack or crystal, or taking opiates, or going gambling, or whatever addictive behavior you find yourself struggling with. Last, but not least: Be patient with yourself, but be persistent!

Sample Cost/Benefit Analysis (CBA)

The table below is an example of a Cost Benefit Analysis. The top-left quadrant lists some benefits while the bottom-left quadrant lists some costs of an addictive or compulsive behavior. On the right are the benefits (top) and costs (bottom) of abstaining or refraining from an addictive or compulsive behavior.

When brainstorming a CBA with the group in a meeting, the final question is, "Which quadrants or squares contain long-term and short-term costs and benefits?" Most groups see that the costs of abstaining are mainly short term and the benefits are longer term. Most also conclude that the costs of using a substance or engaging in compulsive behavior are long term and the benefits of problem behaviors are don't last long.

q

	Addictive/Compulsive Behavior	Abstaining from Add/Comp Behavior
B N E F I T S	Less Anxiety: Social, Job, Relationships	Improved thinking and judgment
	Distraction from/avoidance of problems	Saving money
	The guaranteed, right-now high or buzz	More time for career and other pursuits
	Easier and better sex	Health, fitness self-care improve
	I'm smarter, funnier, more fun	Relationships, reputation, improve
	Socializing is easier/better	Better able to live my values, reach my goals
	Life is more fun with more highs	Outlook, resilience, persistence improve
	I'm controlling how I feel	Realistic about control of outcomes, feelings
C O S T S	Job performance, career problems	Tolerating, accepting discomforts of daily life
	Legal problems	No guaranteed, right-now high or buzz
	Money problems	Learning to socialize without the substance
	Health problems	Losing friends and making new friends
	Relationship problems	Learning to have honest relationships
	Life is less and less fun	Experiencing failures without the substance
	Social embarrassment, social isolation	Learning to enjoy daily life the substance
	I feel out of control	Avoiding/dealing with unexpected triggers

The human brain. Source: wbur.com 1

This roughed out CBA could be anybody's. What I find important to realize is that compulsive behavior and a substance use do have benefits: lowered anxiety, distraction from boredom and problems, a buzz or feeling of comfort, and so on. Some are also funny. My friend actually remembers being convinced that IQ improved with alcohol. Certainly words came easily, he says, even if they were hurtful and then slurred. Reduced anxiety is my payoff when I binge eat.

Of course, everybody talks about the downside of self-destructive behavior. That's easy to see, as are the benefits of abstaining or refraining from self-destruction.

After white-boarding a CBA generated by a folks at a meeting, a good question or frame to pose to the group is, "Now, can we decide long-term versus short-term costs and benefits. Two things are apparent:

Abstaining requires mostly short-term costs and generates long-term benefits.

Continuing a self-destructive behavior results in mostly long-term costs and short-term benefits.

The CBA looks squarely at real-life consequences, the good and the bad. I hope it helps you make real-life choices day-to-day.

W's Story: High in April, Shot Down in May

Starting at 13

I worked my way down. Early trauma, genetic factors, a taste for risk with or without reward, the crazy in me (maybe you have some, too) -- came together to hijack the me of me. Causes don't really matter to me anymore; I suppose you can apply many deft constructs as to why I became self-destructive and hurt others.

I've had two careers: one in academia, one in business. The first, which began well, ended in a few years when my self-medication with alcohol eliminated my effectiveness. Drinking also meant divorce.

Mix in a young child with cognitive problems caused by a congenital condition. My thoughts, feelings and actions were clearly not good for anybody, but I saw what I did as control.

Then another life—cleaned up haltingly over a year-and-a-half, despite or because of seeing no reason to "give it (control over my thought and actions) up." I began and built a respectable place as a professional, husband, father. I ran for the local School Board. I lost on principle.

The business didn't have the strength or luck to survive the Dotcom bust. I took contractor work at a large technology company. That lasted a couple of years. I jumped back and forth between short contract jobs in both business and academia.

Results

After 18 years, I started drinking again, which led to separation, then another divorce. I was losing both my sons and myself, my whole second life. What a bitch.

There were some good thrills, but lots more spills during my first two lives:

Walking the 4 miles each way (uphill) to the state-run liquor store, I rolled drunk down a steep, gravel-spread track ballast. It was the rural South, two rails shimmering through a dark and deep-green forest in late summer. I swam in place, each fumbling step and pull up the gravel sinking back to its starting place. The sun moved until two other track-walkers stopped. They reached down the bank, black hands joined with mine, to pull me up. We split what I could spare of a my two-liter vodka. They had malt liquors. I was tar-and-soot and thirsty again.

Acute liver failure was a three-month downer. I was told a person must be sober and still living for six months to qualify for a transplant. Nobody suggested that I jump on the list. The consensus: I'd not qualify, one way or the other.

And so on.

Take Three

I'm committed to hope. I don't ask why. Press me, and I say I think it's luck. But it's my perception—four-years on—that I have changed my behavior. People who love me tell me that. Friend and acquaintances—even the package and maintenance guys downstairs—tell me.

My participation in SMART recovery, along with the help of others, has given me a way to interpret this balancing act that is life. It is possible to choose a path, your own path without fear. For too long, my world was comprised of threats that I thought I could fight by devising the perfect whatever in my thoughts, feelings and actions. Or by going AWOL.

It hardly needs saying that I failed at perfection. And I was surprised. That my predicament was the norm for everybody—this did not register with me.

SMART thinking has helped me to accept my imperfection and to realize that, at best, I could gain some control over my own thoughts and actions. It's actually fun to practice patience and persistence because I know they are being helpful to my goal of abstinence from alcohol.

Using SMART tools, along with help (yes, I take prescription drugs) from health professionals, has habituated me to stop, mostly, demanding immediate results and then reacting with frustration, anger and eventually drinking when I don't get the results I irrationally expect. I've stopped believing I can predict what will happen outside of my control. I've stopped, again mostly, reading other people's minds to find out what they think about me. Things like asteroids and rudeness don't bother me as much.

I don't pretend to have the academic understanding required to evaluate the science underlying SMART. Critiques of methods do nothing for me in the here and now. SMART tools are working for me. Maybe I will replace anger-time with to a closer examination of the behavior science. Probably not. But I and others do see me now as thinking more clearly and more creatively about my place and time wherever we are. Certainly, there's more time to write. It's not always a curse that one's job and passion are the same.

My Motivation: Hierarchy of Values or Values Clarification

The first "program aim" of SMART is Building and Maintaining Motivation for ending an undesirable behavior, in my case, drinking. One of the SMART tools I use for structuring or framing motivation is creating a Hierarchy of Values. Simply put, I write down what ideals I value most, and to put them in order of priority.

What I'm saying is that you think about and choose your values, and you strive toward these values (maybe you call them ideals) -- all the while realizing that your values/ideals can never be fully achieved or perfected. Perfectionism has been pernicious in attempting to change the course of my life. Persistence, patience and practice, however, are sometimes difficult but achievable attitudes and activities that can contribute to a sustained, fun abstinence from compulsive and obsessive behaviors or illnesses.

For me, underpinning my striving to live a purposeful, content life is the conviction that hope is a better, more joyful motivator than fear. Whenever and wherever possible, I think and act to achieve what I hope for instead of fleeing what I fear.

Traveling through my years—each can be a full cycle of creative adaptation to recurring changes—I have altered my values and their relative priorities as my environment changed.

Here's an example from a yearly cycle I recorded:

Value	April-June 20XX	July-Sept.. 20XX	Oct.-Dec.20XX.	Jan.-March 20XX
1	Build and rebuild love with family	Relationships: family	Relationships: family/friends	Relationships: family/friends
2	Health: Continue recovery from surgery, practice SMART tools	Health: PT, routine exercise, right diet, practice SMART tools	Health: PT, exercise, diet, recovery, persistence, patience	Health: PT exercise, diet, caretaking, further recover, persistence, patience
3	Integrity: truth telling, helping, more...	Integrity: truth telling, helping, consistency, more	Integrity: truth telling, helping, consistency, more	Integrity: truth telling, helping, dependability, more
4	Creativity: explore employment, volunteering	Creativity: explore employment, volunteering	Creativity: explore employment, volunteering	Creativity: explore employment and recovery
5	Discover fun, my newish city	Try new things, be open to change	Be open to change, keep learning.	Learning and change:: bite off, chew and swallow

Although it may seem that during the sampled year my values were consistent, that's not the case. For one, I set the values, but I struggled with some. I made mistakes, wronged people and myself. Nevertheless, it was a good year, full of progress, purpose and fun. My values motivated and guided my thoughts, feelings and actions, except when they didn't.

Earlier in my life, my values were different. Drinking and shouting high-minded bull about life, for instance, was a value for me. So was making money and building a professional reputation. Who knew those wouldn't work together for me? They did and do for some people. Accepting that fact sometimes sucks. Mostly, though, the act of not drinking sets me free to control my choices and deal with the 99.9n% of the universe whose inertia I cannot alter.

Using Values to Set Goals

How do you make the rubber hit the road as far as values? The SMART tool for that is goal-setting. That is, for every value you have prioritized, can you think of achievable goals that are aligned with that value? For example, under the value Health in my value-set, I decided on the goal of "three-to-four workouts per week."

I created and tested my goal using the SMART Handbook's five-point definition:

- Specific: Yes, I detail "three-to-four workouts."
- Measurable: I count, structure and time my workouts.
- Agreeable: To me, this means two things (neither in the SMART Handbook): One: That the goal is aligned with and/or moves toward a defined value. Two: that the goal be something that results in thoughts and feelings registering as a "high" on my fun-happiness-contentment scale.
- Realistic: Yes, I'm lucky enough to have the time, means and physical ability to complete workouts that haven't yet hurt me.
- Time-bound: A week is seven days.

This is a simple example that works for me right now. Another goal aligned with my value of Health is not so simple. For instance, I have reacted in anger to navigating the healthcare system in New York City, both as a patient advocating for myself, and as a best-I-can-do caretaker/caretake.

The whole two-year experience added up to three surgical procedures—two for me, one for my girlfriend—and long periods of recovery. I've been able to break down this very large undertaking bite-size goals. Or sometimes I react in anger and depression. A short stint in the fetal position sometimes helps me; sometimes a workout is better.

The thing is, tomorrow I'll be walking to my doctor's office through the city and the park, first remembering to fast for a blood test. Great walk, but the new hip causes discomfort and some worries.

If a young person, say 25 to 35, were—in a most un-New-York way—to ask me on the street how I feel about my upcoming trip to the doctor, I'd say, "Totally worth it! But I'm not going to mention the colonoscopy referral she gave me three months ago."

Story 29

Perry Street Workshop
by John L.

Thousands of people, now living all over the world, have found sobriety in a storefront room in New York City's Greenwich Village: the Perry Street Workshop. For me Perry Street will always be Alcoholics Anonymous, my home base no matter where I am. In 2008, as Perry Street celebrated its 50th anniversary, members created a website and a brochure, The Perry Street 50th Year Anniversary Booklet, which is available in pdf format on their website. <50perrystreet.org>

When I revisited Perry Street last year, time stood still. I saw the exact spot where I had sat at my first A.A. meeting, 46 years ago. Almost nothing had changed. The podium; the chair arrangement; the hand-lettered Steps, Traditions and Serenity Prayer, were the same. The only thing missing was cigarette smoke.

I remember my first meeting very well, a Thursday beginners meeting in early January 1968. I was in bad shape, having almost died in terminal alcohol withdrawal. My friend Andy and another A.A. member helped me walk across town, from my apartment in Manhattan's East Village. When I sat down, I was very weak and shaking violently, my teeth were chattering, and I was unable to focus my eyes. People said I should go immediately to a hospital, but I refused, saying that I was there for the meeting — so they covered me with overcoats and set an electric space heater in front of me. I identified completely with the speaker, a man in his thirties. Everything came together. I experienced hope and an intense desire to live. If the others in the room had survived, then so could I.

That weekend Andy had a relapse and disappeared, but I was not alone. I had a meeting list and phone numbers. Although Andy never did achieve lasting sobriety, he saved my life. He was the only sponsor I have ever had. In those days, at least at Perry Street, sponsors were regarded as optional, intended mainly to help the newcomer in early sobriety. They were not, as now, supposed to be long-term, all-purpose counsellors or therapists.

I'll pass over the story of my physical recovery, since I've told that in another article [link to "Physical Recovery"] and concentrate on memories of my first year — what in AA has changed and what has remained the same.

In 1968, as now, almost all meetings at Perry Street (except beginners meetings) were closed — for alcoholics only. This lends them a sense of candor and intimacy that is lost when meetings are open to the general public. Anything a recovering alcoholic discusses, in the company of other alcoholics, can be relevant. I remember a small afternoon meeting at Perry Street — most of us newcomers — where one young man shared that, in the euphoria of his new sobriety, he had gotten a $15 haircut. We laughed and identified completely. (For perspective, that $15 haircut in 1968 would cost many times that much now.)

Sometimes discussions led into what I call "recreational arguments" — energetic, but good-natured. Some of the bones of contention were doctors, the Steps, and religion. Those who preened themselves on their piety, or even worse, "Higher Power, whom I choose to call [dramatic pause] God", would likely be answered by someone who hated religion, especially the Catholic Church, which had blasted his life. At a meeting of the New Day group in Greenwich Village, my friend Bruce responded to an egregious display of piety by saying, "I'm in AA to be sober; I'm not here to be good."

As pungently free as discussions could be, the Perry Street meetings were orderly. It was believed important to maintain a tone conducive to sobriety. Meetings never ran over the time allotted; if a meeting was supposed to end at 9 p.m., it did, even if someone was cut off in mid-sentence. "No souls saved after Midnight." People did not interrupt each other, although people were tactfully prevented from speaking too long or running off the rails.

Active alcoholics were welcome at meetings, but only so long as they behaved themselves; if they created a disturbance, the chair would tell them that if they did it again, they would be escorted from the meeting. They usually remained silent. I remember one occasion when "escorting" was necessary; it was done, gently but firmly, by a man who had been a professional bouncer before sobriety.

I had been sober for perhaps two months when a thoroughly disreputable old man showed up. In those days people didn't arrive from detox centers, but sometimes right from the Bowery. He was not only ragged and dirty and unshaven — he smelled bad, and people moved away from him. Vaguely believing that I could do a 12th Step, I spoke to him and did my best to carry the message of sobriety. Week after week he would show up, and I always spoke to him. Then one day he showed up: clean, shaven, well groomed, wearing a new suit, and looking many years younger. He looked so proud! I think I was never happier for the happiness of another human being.

It wasn't always sweetness and light. Beginning in 1965, I was heavily involved in the antiwar movement, until my activism was curtailed by physical collapse in the final year of drinking. In August 1968 the Democratic Party convention was held in Chicago, with two peace candidates: Senators George McGovern and Eugene McCarthy. The Chicago police, under the direction of Mayor Daley — violently hostile to the antiwar movement — rioted, attacking protesters, photographers, reporters, and bystanders. In the morning of 29 August 1968 the police invaded the campaign headquarters of Senator McCarthy, destroying equipment and brutally striking campaign workers with their nightsticks. Some of the workers were even dragged out of bed before being beaten. At this time I had been sober for half a year and was horrified. At a meeting, with tears streaming down my face, I shared my distress — but for less than a minute. All hell broke loose, as soon as people realized that I was against the war in Vietnam. They furiously shouted me down, and some of them leaped from their seats to attack me. Two older women led me outside, and then to their apartment, which was nearby. Perhaps a half dozen others also left with us, and we held an alternate AA meeting there. They comforted me, and I realized that I had friends — but also realized that there are limits to AA discussion, politics being one of them.

Another newcomer in the Village groups was a retired army colonel. No matter what he started out talking about, he always concluded by saying that we had to have Victory In Vietnam. No one ever objected. I would remain silent, wishing that he and everyone else in the room would stay sober, but not sure I'd mind watching him walk in front of a truck. Live and Let Live!

Perry Street members were heterogeneous, although, as expected for Greenwich Village, there were writers, artists, intellectuals, gay men, lesbians, political radicals, and sundry nonconformists.

On the whole, there was an absence of religiosity. Some used the Steps, but others ignored them, and some actively hated them. On the wall were hand-lettered Steps and Traditions; the header of the former read: "12 Suggested Steps" — where the central and longest word is Suggested. The significance of this occurred to me only recently, when viewing the Perry Street brochure. All other versions of the Steps that I've seen on AA walls omit the most important word of all: Suggested. I would guess that most of the Perry Street members back in the 1960s and 1970s rejected the "suggestion" and simply ignored the Steps.

All meetings ended with the Lord's Prayer, which bothered me as I began to heal, physically and psychologically. In retrospect, I think that most members had no enthusiasm for the LP, but simply thought that AA meetings had to end that way. I and a handful of others defiantly remained seated when the others got up to recite the LP. Years later I wrote and circulated "A Proposal to Eliminate the Lord's Prayer from AA Meetings". [link here]

All Perry Street meetings, as well as the midnight meetings held on West 23rd Street, stressed the 24-Hour Plan, staying away from the First Drink. In my first year I must have heard thousands of times, "Stay away from the First Drink." "It's the First Drink that gets you drunk." "Don't drink, no matter what." Most importantly, "You don't have to drink!" These are what I needed to hear.

On weekend evenings, people from meetings all over Manhattan would go to a restaurant near Perry Street — Spiro's, a large restaurant on 7th Avenue. Spiro's would then be virtually all AA. There was a very long table that could seat perhaps 30 or more, and many smaller tables and booths. It was the custom that anyone could sit at the long table, as though already introduced to the others. The booths would be filled by those with common interests, including freethinkers, gay men, and those who qualified for Mensa.

A good friend during my first few months was Bob, a freethinker, gay man, and hemophiliac. We and like-minded guys spent many dozens of hours in booths at Spiro's — talking about all kinds of things. We sometimes made fun of the Steps or Big Book religiosity, but always respected sobriety and the Fellowship. One day it was announced that Bob had begun bleeding uncontrollably and was in St. Vincent's Hospital. In the next two days more than 80 AA members donated blood to help him. I did myself, although I was still so thin that the nurse wasn't sure she could get a pint out of me. But it was too late: he bled to death. There was no Factor VIII then. Although Bob had despised religion, he was given a Roman Catholic funeral, well attended by AA members.

Death was a constant companion in recovery. I remember announcements of people who died in relapses, and others who died sober of old age. In my first year I frequently went to weekend midnight meetings, which I liked because the people there were fighting for sobriety, not dabbling in "spirituality". A young man, who had been in for a few years, always talked to me, and we were getting to know each other. Then one night I was told that he had died — which hardly seemed possible, since he was strong and vigorously healthy. He was a classic periodic drunk, someone who can stay away from a drink for a long time, but for whom a First Drink means immediate disaster. The man who told me put it: "He drank until his heart stopped." Less than three days.

The worst thing about the Perry Street meetings was the

smoke, especially at crowded evening meetings. They were gas chambers. Just being in the room meant inhaling the equivalent of a half pack of cigarettes. Perhaps this is why I don't recall going through nicotine withdrawal, even though I stopped smoking at the same time I stopped drinking. As my sobriety progressed, this bothered me, for a reason that is seldom discussed. We stay sober by not picking up the First Drink. But being in a smoky room is like puffing on the First Cigarette plus several more, thus triggering a craving for one of the most addictive substances known: nicotine. Although I didn't entirely stop going to Perry Street meetings, I increasingly went to meetings where there was less smoke or none. According to the 50th Year Anniversary Booklet, it wasn't until the 1990s that Perry Street finally banned smoking.

At Village meetings, an announcement was made: "If you have had a drink today, or a mood-changer, we ask that you not take part in discussion — but please stay around and talk to someone after the meeting." I'm not sure those were the exact words, but they are the gist of it. On this issue, AA was far ahead of the medical establishment, which maintained that the new generation of tranquillizers (Valium and Librium) were not addictive and had none of the terrible toxicities of the old tranquilizers (like Miltown). We knew better, because we had heard one person after another describe the harmful effects of Librium or Valium, and the sheer hell of breaking addiction to them. Obviously, this is an area of controversy. My own sobriety entails the avoidance of all mood-changing drugs, whether street or pharmaceutical, whether prescribed by a physician or not. I think it's deplorable that many alcoholics are now put on psychiatric drugs before they even leave detox.

Some things change, and some remain the same. Perry Street and most AA groups no longer allow smoking and have replaced the Lord's Prayer with the Serenity Prayer (or something else or nothing). That's good. I personally think some of AA's intimacy and intensity was lost when boisterous practices from California spread across the country in the 1970s: frequent applause and the shouting of greetings and various interjections. You can't listen and applaud at the same time. To me, the emotional commitment of saying: "I'm John, and

185

I am an alcoholic." is lost when the rest of the room yells, "Hi-ya, John!"

I am no longer young, and no longer middle-aged, but I'm still in AA and still sober. Thank you, Perry Street!

John L. celebrates 46 years from his last drink in February 2014. He has a section in his website: Alcoholism: Recovery Without Religiosity.

<paganpressbooks.com/jpl/ALK-FREE.HTM> (Case sensitive)

CONTRIBUTORS

1. Njon Sanders When I started my current recovery journey, I remember being excited and oddly hopeful. This feeling was consistently validated in progress via baby steps (and a few leaps). Early on, I started a new LifeRing meeting in my area. I then started a few more and shortly thereafter became 0a Regional Rep, helping to onboard and network new meetings. Soon after, I joined the Board of Directors which I chaired for two years.

I still find benefit in my local LifeRing meeting, but I no longer consider recovery to be synonymous with meeting attendance. My recovery lifestyle is no longer limited to what are commonly considered "traditional Recovery settings". Recovery is now about having a life!

I've been a featured speaker at CCAR's Multiple Pathways of Recovery conference since its inception in 2016. This coupled with my numerous volunteer initiatives has raised my confidence level globally and I've taken on a mentor role within my professional community.

I currently chair the San Francisco Mental Health Board / Behavioral Health Commission. My focus here is promoting integrative, holistic services to better support consumers whose needs have been previously unaddressed. As I term-out of this role, I'm simultaneously developing a podcast dedicated to behavioral health and local politics. I'm also taking the preliminary steps at a run at public office.

2. Mike K. I was born in 1937. I attended Thomas Jefferson School in Kirkwood, MO and earned a BA from Harvard College 1959. I also attended various business management advanced courses at Washington University. I was Married from 1961-1979 to my first wife, and from 1979 to present to my second wife. I have three sons and two daughters from 44 to 57 years old

From 1959 to 2001 I was employed in the textile industry at two companies. I held positions of increasing responsibility topping out as president of a 500 employee manufacturing company with five plants in the U.S. and one in Mexico and one in Honduras. From 2001 to 2010, I formed my own consulting business which served global clients. I have traveled extensively throughout the US, Europe, Latin America and Asia.

I live in an exurb of St. Louis with my wife and youngest daughter. I am physically healthy, spiritually growing, and emotionally maturing.

3. Craig Whalley After retiring in 2009 following almost 40 years as a bookseller in Port Angeles, WA, I moved to Berkeley, CA, and devoted as much time as possible to LifeRing Secular Recovery until I returned to Port Angeles in 2017. I still give what time I can to helping LifeRing grow, thrive, and offer its approach to as many people as possible. I now convene a local meeting, co-convene another and also oversee a large and active online email group.

4. Adam Sledd is a person in long-term recovery and a public recovery advocate. He is a father, husband, student, counselor and recovery educator. His formula for recovery is a balance of work, activism, family, and friends.

8. Nancy was born in Canada in 1944. She has worked as a journalist, teacher, author and editor of both fiction and non-fiction books. She currently lives in Launceston, Tasmania with her partner Howard and Billy the Kid (cat). She has been sober since September 2012 and she is happy.

9. Dennis Meeks I initially got sober in 1989 and remained free from alcohol for almost 23 years. However, I became addicted to opioids for the last years of that period of alcohol abstinence and when the pills ran out, the door to the liquor store reopened . For approximately three years I binged, sometimes for weeks at a time. I stumbled across LifeRing online during this time and finally quit drinking on June 29, 2013. I could not have done it without the compassionate encouragement of the LR mail group to which I belong.

10. Philip Henderson lives in Belfast, Northern Ireland

11. Bobbi Campbell Bobbi, an Oregon native, is now living happily ever after as a Southern California transplant with her husband Richard and goes out of her way to help people whenever and in whatever way possible.

14. Mary Lee Peterson I was born in Denver, Colorado, in 1947. I was a 'religious' girl so I drank very little until I moved to California in 1969. I was always a cheap date because of a combination of genetics. My Swedish father was an alcoholic and died of alcohol poisoning in 1948; my mother and maternal grandfather were allergic to alcohol. I spent years drinking only one glass of wine once or twice a month. Then in 2003 I lost my job and quickly fell into drinking daily. In 2009 I realized I couldn't stop on my own. I enrolled into the Kaiser Chemical Dependence Program where I found LifeRing. I never would have made it without the support of such an active and supportive group. In 2010 I returned to Denver and was thrilled that LifeRing was there too! I now proudly convene LifeRing meetings in Denver.

15. Richard Campbell is happily semi-retired, after a career in healthcare financial services, and living extra-happily in Torrance, California, with his lovely wife, Bobbi.

16. Mary S. was born in NJ 1950; started drinking 1989; married 1994; moved to CA 1997; got sober 2004; moved to NM 2004; divorced 2013; and lived happily ever after.

18. Steve Snyder is a survivor of various forms of child abuse and encourages male survivors to get the support they need.

19. m.k. is a retired university fundraising manager. she credits her involvement with LifeRing in giving her recovery from addiction to alcohol serious traction. she lives in Salt Lake City where she is active in the local recovery community and is engaged in the business of living life to the fullest.

20. Hilary I was born in London 1949. Diploma in Art and

Design Textiles and Photography MA Textiles Teaching (Art) Skelmersdale College Edge Hill University Escola International Sao Lourenco Exhibitions of digital art in UK, Portugal and India. Now I'm retired, with part time childcare of six grandchildren, including two sets of twins!

21. Tim Reith is a former intrepid LifeRing board secretary.

22. Robert Stump I have lived in the San Francisco Bay Area my whole life. Born in 1952, I started using drugs (including alcohol) once I left high school. After some experimenting, I settled on my drug of choice and drank for the next 35 years. I finally found sobriety through the Kaiser's treatment program and LifeRing (my world view would not support the 12-step model) in 2006. I now live a happy and quiet life with my wife and our five adult children.

23. James Ringland is a retired statistician living with his wife, Karen, in Oakland, California. He was born and schooled in the Midwest, receiving his PhD from the University of Illinois in 1980. He then came to the Bay Area of California, applying his mathematics to issues in operations and systems analysis, engineering safety, and reliability. Most, but not all, was in the support of national defense. He was active in LifeRing primarily from 2007 through 2010. At various times during that period he convened a Recovery by Choice workbook group in Berkeley, California, acted as the organization's secretary and served on the Board of Directors. He loves Western classical music, mostly Schubert back to the Renaissance, but with some interests later. Before and since retirement, he has been an active hiker and backpacker, visiting California's Big Sur and the Sierra Nevada areas most, but enjoying trips farther afield.

24. Byron Kerr I am 66 years old. I live and work in Silicon Valley at one of the tech giants (hint, 1+ one hundred zeros). I have three adult daughters from a 35 year marriage that ended years ago. I am approximately 7 1/2 years sober - I don't calculate to the hour and minute.

Becoming active in LifeRing has been extremely gratifying for me. I appear to have some skill in starting new meetings, finding new convenors, and repeating. In 2018, I was appointed executive director of LifeRing. Finding my replacement is one of my main goals.

26. Patty was born in 1961 in Baltimore, Maryland, and grew up in a small town in the northern part of the state. In 1991, having had enough of cold winters and wishing to further her drinking career (preferably outdoors), she packed her pug and whatever else she could fit into her Beretta and headed south to St. Petersburg, Florida. Life was Good, until it wasn't anymore (read for yourself), but she has been continuously sober since 2006, and is now happily married, with six dogs, and contentedly employed at a local branch of a national nonprofit in St. Petersburg.

27. CA Edington is a semi-retired teacher as well as proofreader, narrator, and hypnotist living in Sapporo, Japan, with her two cats. She is the only non- Japanese in Sapporo Symphony Chorus. She has 21 years of sobriety, all through LifeRing (formerly SOS).

28. John Lauritsen was born and raised in Nebraska. He attended Harvard College (AB 1963), majoring in Social Relations (Sociology, Anthropology and Psychology). In New York City he worked as a market research executive, writing on the side. He was in the antiwar movement since 1965 and the gay liberation movement since July 1969. He founded Pagan Press in 1982. For a decade, beginning in 1985, John was a leading writer for the New York Native, which was then the foremost gay paper. He has twelve books to his credit. John dates his alcoholism from his first bender in 1958 to his last drink in 1968. He considers himself a loyal, but by no means uncritical, member of AA. John now lives in Dorchester, Massachusetts.

45509378R00113

Made in the USA
San Bernardino, CA
29 July 2019